Prompt Power

Prompt Power

The Hidden Art of Communicating With AI

Elena Marceau

Mindful Pages

Published in 2026

ISBN: 9789374124987(PB)
ISBN: 9789374121443 (eBook)

Published by

Mindful Pages
Imprint of Alpha Editions LLC
312 W. 2nd St #1834
Casper, WY 82601, USA

This book was developed using advanced writing tools to support the drafting and ideation process. All content has been thoughtfully curated, refined, and reviewed to ensure quality and relevance.

Content

Introduction
The Hidden Art of Communicating with Intelligence

There is a quiet revolution underway, and its currency is language. Not the language of poetry or politics, but the kind that sits between human intent and machine interpretation — the prompt. In a world where machines can summarise books, simulate dialogue, and generate code, it is easy to believe that human effort has been reduced to the press of a button. Yet the paradox is stark: the more "intelligent" our systems become, the more our words must do the heavy lifting. A single adjective can tilt an answer; a missing constraint can waste an afternoon; an unexamined assumption can turn assistance into error at scale. What we write — or fail to write — now determines not merely what a machine says, but what it believes we meant.

The prompt is no longer a casual query. It is a clause in an invisible contract between human intention and statistical reasoning. Behind every response lies a negotiation — a dance between clarity and probability, between what we mean and what the model infers. Each word becomes both instruction and wager, an assertion of what we know and an exposure of what we do not. To prompt well is to legislate the boundaries of understanding itself. And to prompt poorly is to surrender precision to chance.

This book begins with that paradox and treats it not as a novelty of technology but as a mirror of human communication. The prompt, in truth, is ancient. It inherits the lineage of the question, the brief, the scientific hypothesis, the legal clause, the prayer. It is the act of asking for something to be made real through words. What has changed is scale and immediacy: the fact that language now directs engines of computation capable of producing volumes of thought-like text in seconds. We have, quite suddenly, become rhetoricians for machines. But most of us are speaking without a grammar.

The purpose of *Prompt Power* is to teach that grammar — not as a technical manual but as a philosophy of expression and accountability. It is a book about writing, judgement, and the ethics of delegation. It begins not with tools but with thought: what does it mean to make intent operational? How do we encode clarity, constraint, and conscience into our instructions? How do we expose our own biases before they are amplified at scale? To master prompting is to reclaim authorship in a world of algorithmic authors. It is to learn how to make language both instrument and safeguard.

Before algorithms, there were scribes and contracts. When merchants of the Renaissance codified agreements, every clause mattered. A misplaced comma could shift ownership; an ambiguous term could undo a fortune. The art of drafting was an art of foresight — to anticipate misunderstanding before it occurred. Prompting, too, demands such discipline. Every word carries latent probability; every omission leaves room for misinterpretation. In this sense, a prompt is a contract: negotiated in language, enforced by probability, and audited by outcome. It defines scope, assigns obligation, and sets expectation. The clearer the contract, the fewer the disputes.

But unlike parchment agreements, prompts are living documents. They evolve through dialogue, through trial and revision. Each exchange with an AI is a rehearsal of reasoning: a hypothesis tested, an instruction refined, a result measured. To prompt well, one must think experimentally, not declaratively. The writer becomes both scientist and advocate — designing linguistic experiments that probe the edges of machine understanding. The prompt ceases to be a command; it becomes an inquiry, disciplined and repeatable. That is why this book draws as much from law and science as from linguistics. To think in prompts is to think in systems.

What distinguishes the adept from the amateur is not access to better technology, but to better mental models. The untrained user asks once and accepts whatever comes. The skilled prompter asks as a means of discovery — adjusting variables, testing boundaries, measuring uncertainty. Each iteration is a microcosm of the scientific method: hypothesis, test, observation, revision. In this light, prompting is not a trick or "hack" but a literacy. And like all literacies, it shapes thought itself.

Language, at its best, is a form of stewardship. It binds collective understanding and transmits culture across generations. Now it also binds our digital creations to human values. Yet language is imperfect; it reflects bias, hierarchy, omission. When machines learn from human text, they inherit our asymmetries — gendered assumptions, cultural defaults, moral shortcuts. The prompt becomes both mirror and lever: it can reveal bias or reinforce it, expose complexity or flatten it. To prompt ethically is to intervene consciously in that inheritance. It is to accept that every instruction carries the weight of worldview.

Consider a medical assistant trained on biased data: a vague or culturally narrow prompt might yield advice that endangers. Consider a hiring model: an unexamined adjective — "assertive," "polished," "native-like" — could tilt opportunity. In each case, prompting is not a peripheral act but the moment where human values meet algorithmic inference. The ethical frontier of artificial intelligence is written in the small print of our instructions.

This is why the book insists on discipline. It argues for a method — plan, test, record, reflect — as a safeguard against our own complacency. Tools change quickly; principles endure. The chapters that follow equip readers not with recipes but with reasoning habits. You will learn to draft prompts as contracts (Chapter 1), to run dialogues as experiments (Chapter 2), to choose words with surgical precision (Chapter 3), to read replies through psychological insight (Chapter 4), to confront bias and power (Chapter 5), to unlock creativity through constraint (Chapter 6), to apply these lessons across writing, coding, and design (Chapter 7), and finally to understand the emerging "prompt economy" — a world where language itself becomes infrastructure (Chapter 8). The book closes not with prediction but with practice, offering a durable discipline for the human future of prompting.

There is urgency here. The interface — that thin membrane of text — is now the workplace of millions. Through it, policies are drafted, lessons designed, therapies guided, art conceived. Every exchange leaves a linguistic footprint that shapes systems downstream. To treat prompts as casual utterances is to misunderstand their power.

We are writing, daily, the operating language of intelligence itself. The question is whether we do so with awareness or by accident.

The tools we use will continue to evolve, but the principle will not: the quality of outcomes will always trace back to the quality of questions. The danger is not that machines will think for us, but that we will stop thinking carefully before we speak to them. This is the paradox at the heart of our moment. Intelligence — artificial or human — begins with articulation. To command clarity from systems, we must first command clarity from ourselves.

Perhaps, then, prompting is less about communication with machines than about rediscovering what makes language powerful between people: precision, empathy, accountability. These are not technical virtues but moral ones. In learning to write better prompts, we are learning to think more honestly — to define our intent, name our bias, and measure our effect. Prompting, at its highest form, becomes a discipline of thought.

So this book is not about automation; it is about authorship. It does not celebrate the replacement of human labour but the refinement of human intention. To prompt well is to think in clauses, test like a scientist, and speak like a human being who understands that words shape worlds. That is the promise — and the demand — of *Prompt Power*.

Chapter 1
The Prompt Is a Contract

Imagine standing before an architect with only this instruction: *Build me something impressive.* No location, no dimensions, no budget, no purpose. The result might dazzle or disappoint, but it would almost certainly miss the mark. Now transpose that vagueness into a conversation with a machine—one that does not truly *understand* you, but instead calculates what is most probable given your words. The outcome will mirror your precision or your carelessness, amplified at machine speed. A vague prompt is an open-ended brief to an indifferent architect: what returns is random grandeur, not relevance.

Every day, across industries and disciplines, people issue such prompts without realising they are drafting contracts. The writer expects insight, the model delivers approximation, and somewhere in the probabilistic fog between question and response, intent is lost. Yet when a prompt is written with clarity and rigour, the relationship transforms. The exchange becomes a binding agreement—terms defined, scope delimited, deliverables measurable. *The Prompt Is a Contract* is not a metaphor of convenience; it is the governing principle of intelligent communication.

At its heart lies a simple truth: intent precedes instruction. Every prompt encodes a purpose, a scope, and a success criterion—whether stated or not. When those remain implicit, the model improvises. It fills the void with its statistical instincts, shaped by millions of patterns from human language, none of which belong to you. That is stochastic drift: the slow, invisible migration of your request away from your true intention. The difference between "summarise this report" and "produce a 200-word executive summary highlighting financial risk factors and mitigation strategies" is not cosmetic. It is the difference between suggestion and specification, between hoping for understanding and ensuring it.

In law, ambiguity breeds litigation; in prompting, it breeds error. Both arise from the same neglect: the failure to define terms before the work begins. Lawyers do not write clauses because they distrust their clients—they write them because they respect the unpredictable nature of interpretation. Similarly, prompting well is not about mistrusting machines, but about anticipating their limits. When a system trained on probability meets an instruction written in generalities, the outcome is not intelligence but improvisation. And improvisation, at scale, is risk.

To prompt with precision is therefore to accept responsibility. It is to recognise that the words we choose determine the boundaries of reasoning. Constraints—inputs, formats, exclusions—are not obstacles but safeguards. They function like contractual clauses, delineating what the model *may* and *may not* do. A prompt that specifies "respond in JSON format with three key recommendations and their rationale" imposes structure. It transforms creative chaos into measurable output. Far from stifling creativity, constraint enables focus. It converts potential energy into directed work.

The power of such constraints can be quantified. In practice, prompts rich in explicit boundaries produce results that are not only more accurate but more efficient. Time saved compounds across iterations; clarity compounds across collaboration. The professional learns this as a discipline: every instruction must contain its own guardrails. The novice learns it the hard way—through drift, misfire, and repetition. The distinction mirrors that between amateur correspondence and legal drafting: both use language, but only one is accountable to outcomes.

Yet even the most explicit contract cannot foresee every ambiguity. Models, when uncertain, fall back on priors—statistical defaults formed by exposure to language at scale. These defaults are powerful, but also perilous. Ask for "a neutral summary," and you inherit the model's hidden assumptions about neutrality. Request "a balanced view," and you invoke a distribution of balance that may privilege what was most common in the training data, not what is most just. Small wording changes—"evaluate" versus "describe," "risk" versus "challenge"—can shift the entire distribution of responses. The responsible prompter therefore learns to surface and neutralise these hidden defaults, not through paranoia but through explicitness. Ambiguity cannot be eliminated, but it can be managed as risk.

Risk management in prompting follows the same principles that govern every disciplined field: identification, estimation, mitigation. First, detect where ambiguity lives—verbs, adjectives, scope. Then estimate its potential impact: what happens if the model interprets this differently? Finally, mitigate it through specification—define terms, set thresholds, anchor expectations. The process may sound meticulous, even pedantic, but so does drafting an airworthiness checklist or a research protocol. Precision is not bureaucracy; it is insurance.

No contract, however, is complete without mechanisms of enforcement. In language as in law, promises must be verified. The final dimension of this chapter—*Verification and Remedies*—turns prompting from a craft into a discipline. A good prompt does not end with a request; it embeds its own test. Verification prompts act as acceptance criteria: "Confirm that your answer includes all cited sources," "Summarise how your reasoning aligns with the original question." Red-teaming loops introduce deliberate challenge—probing for error before the error propagates. In this way, language becomes both instrument and audit trail. Each interaction can be measured, not merely admired.

The result is a closed circuit of reliability: intent defined, obligations stated, ambiguity managed, verification built in. This is the architecture of dependable prompting. It is not glamorous, but it is transformative. Those who master it move from hoping for insight to guaranteeing it. They understand that clarity is not a personality trait but a professional ethic.

The implications stretch beyond artificial intelligence. Contracts, at their essence, are expressions of trust engineered into language. They bind human complexity to predictable consequence. When we prompt well, we are rehearsing that same discipline—turning fleeting thought into accountable instruction. In doing so, we reclaim something timeless: the human ability to make meaning precise.

This chapter, then, is an invitation to take language seriously again. To treat words not as decoration, but as design. To realise that the prompt is not an incantation that conjures intelligence, but a legal and logical structure that governs it. By its end, you will learn how to write prompts that read like well-drafted contracts—clear in purpose, firm in scope, resilient against misunderstanding. You will see how explicitness liberates rather than confines, and how careful language can transform stochastic possibility into dependable intelligence.

Every intelligent system, human or artificial, is only as trustworthy as the agreements that shape its behaviour. The prompt *is* that agreement. To master it is to step from conversation into control, from experimentation into authorship. The clauses you write today are the rules by which tomorrow's machines will think.

Intent Before Instruction

In January 1986, NASA's engineers gathered in a conference room at the Kennedy Space Center, Florida, to debate whether the Space Shuttle *Challenger* should launch. Temperatures had dropped below freezing overnight; the O-ring seals on the solid rocket boosters had never been tested under such conditions. Morton Thiokol's engineers warned of danger but were instructed by managers to "put their recommendation in writing." Their memo, hastily phrased and lacking explicit thresholds or quantified risk criteria, left just enough ambiguity for optimism to prevail. The shuttle launched. Seventy-three seconds later, it disintegrated. The failure was not purely mechanical. It was linguistic — a tragedy of intent lost in translation. The engineers had an intuition; the managers needed a guarantee. Between those two, clarity collapsed.

Every act of instruction — from an aerospace directive to a digital prompt — carries an encoded intent. Whether written to a human team or an algorithmic model, language declares purpose, scope, and standards of success. The difficulty lies not in possessing intent but in articulating it precisely enough to survive interpretation. Words, like circuits, have tolerances. Too loose, and meaning drifts; too tight, and flexibility vanishes. The art lies in defining the purpose clearly while leaving sufficient room for execution. It is here that prompting, like contracting, becomes an exercise in foresight.

A prompt, properly conceived, is not a command but a commitment. It binds two reasoning systems — human and machine — to a shared expectation. Yet most prompts today are issued as if to an omniscient being: brief, vague, and overconfident. "Write a summary." "Generate ideas." "Analyse this data." Such instructions are open invitations to stochastic drift: the model's internal probabilities wander to fill the gaps our language leaves behind. The result may be eloquent, even impressive, but it is misaligned with the task's true aim. To prevent that drift, we must translate intention into structure, much as a contract translates trust into enforceable terms.

In 2003, the British Medical Journal published an internal review of clinical reporting errors. The majority, investigators found, stemmed from *ambiguous instructions* during data transcription — "record all adverse events" being interpreted differently across teams and sites. The lesson was not about medicine alone. It showed that when a request lacks measurable boundaries, interpreters — human or statistical — substitute their own. The misalignment multiplies downstream, distorting evidence, wasting time, and in high-stakes contexts, risking harm. The cure is explicitness: specifying *what counts* and *what satisfies.*

Intent is the north star of any instruction. But clarity of intent depends on separation between *ends* and *means.* Ends define purpose: *what success looks like.* Means define method: *how to get there.* Confusing the two leads to contradictions. A manager asking a model to "generate a concise report that persuades the board" collapses analysis and rhetoric into one demand. Better to separate: first, extract facts; then, produce persuasive framing. When ends and means merge, evaluation becomes impossible; one cannot test whether persuasion worked if the factual ground is already bent. Clear contracts, and clear prompts, preserve that distinction.

In research methodology, this separation is codified as hypothesis versus procedure. Karl Popper, writing in *The Logic of Scientific Discovery* (1959), insisted that a hypothesis must be falsifiable — that is, testable against observation. The same principle applies to prompting. A prompt should, ideally, yield an answer that can be *judged.* "Explain this algorithm" is open-ended; "Explain this algorithm in 200 words suitable for an undergraduate reader, using one analogy and one limitation" is testable. The difference is not verbosity but verifiability. Language becomes a tool of measurement.

Testability does not mean rigidity. The most resilient contracts include mechanisms for adaptation. In 2019, DeepMind's AlphaFold team in London reframed their internal instructions for protein-structure prediction. Early experiments faltered because the problem statements were too broad: "Predict folding for unseen proteins." By narrowing intent — defining measurable success as *distance accuracy within a specific benchmark set* — performance surged. The model improved because the prompt became an evaluation scaffold, not a wish list. Clarity enabled iteration.

There is, however, a counterpoint worth noting. Excessive specificity can strangle innovation. In 1957, IBM's Thomas Watson Jr. insisted on rigid procedural documentation for software teams, believing precision guaranteed reliability. It did — but it also slowed development to a crawl. Creativity requires a margin of interpretive freedom. The balance lies in aligning clarity with context: specify outcomes where risk is high, leave latitude where exploration adds value. Contracts, legal or linguistic, must scale their precision to the stakes.

Consider how the same principle governs diplomacy. The 1998 Good Friday Agreement in Belfast, brokered between the British and Irish governments, succeeded not by maximal precision but by *strategic ambiguity*. Certain terms — "decommissioning," "consent" — were deliberately left elastic to allow parties with incompatible worldviews to sign the same document. In that context, vagueness was a feature, not a flaw. It bought peace. But ambiguity succeeds only where shared goodwill ensures constructive interpretation. Machines, lacking goodwill, default to probability. Ambiguity in prompting is thus pure entropy. Where humans can infer spirit, machines can only compute syntax.

In prompting, as in law, every word carries a shadow cost. Ambiguity forces downstream renegotiation: clarifications, retries, rework. Each re-iteration compounds inefficiency. Studies at Microsoft Research (2024) found that "clarity-first prompting" — frontloading intent, scope, and format — reduced revision cycles by over 40% in cross-functional teams using generative systems for documentation. The savings were not merely temporal; user satisfaction rose because results matched mental models on the first pass. The correlation is intuitive yet profound: the time invested in defining intent pays back in accuracy and trust.

This is the essence of "clarity up front." It transforms language from reactive correction into proactive design. When professionals invest in phrasing — defining not only *what* they want but *how they will recognise it* — they reduce the cost of uncertainty. They also make their reasoning auditable. A well-structured prompt leaves a trail of logic: it shows why an answer exists, not merely what it is. That transparency is the first defence against automation bias — the human tendency to trust fluent nonsense.

The motif of *contract* recurs here with purpose. A contract exists because humans are unreliable narrators of their own intent. So are we when we speak to machines. We overestimate shared context, underestimate ambiguity, and assume alignment where none exists. The written prompt, like a legal instrument, compensates for that human weakness by freezing meaning into text. Once written, it can be tested, improved, and replicated. Clarity becomes portable knowledge.

Intent, once formalised, also unlocks accountability. When an instruction produces error, one can trace whether the fault lay in the input or the interpretation. This diagnostic clarity is transformative. It shifts the culture of prompting from superstition — "maybe the model misunderstood me" — to governance: "I see where my specification failed." In effect, every prompt becomes an artefact of design. Its language embodies hypotheses about how intelligence behaves. Its success or failure teaches us not just about systems, but about ourselves.

Yet even with intent sharpened and outcomes testable, there remains a subtle risk: assuming that clarity is self-evident. What feels explicit to the writer may not be explicit to the interpreter. The anthropologist Clifford Geertz once remarked that culture is "an interpretive system in which meanings are public but understanding is individual." The same holds true here. Prompts, like cultures, depend on shared frames. Without feedback loops — explicit confirmation of interpretation — even the best-designed contract can fail silently. Therefore, defining intent must be followed by validating comprehension. Ask: *What did you understand this to mean?* Only then does instruction become communication.

A well-formed prompt mirrors a well-structured negotiation. It defines purpose, specifies scope, clarifies deliverables, and anticipates dispute. It embodies respect — not only for the system's limits but for the complexity of meaning itself. It assumes that language is an imperfect bridge, and that precision is the moral duty of anyone who builds across it. That ethic, more than any technique, distinguishes a responsible practitioner from a casual user.

The final test of intent is not elegance but consequence. Does the prompt, when executed, produce what you meant — or merely what you said? Does it minimise drift, or merely disguise it under fluency? The challenge, for every professional and researcher now working with intelligent systems, is to ask before they instruct: *What am I actually trying to achieve, and how will I know when I have achieved it?* The question is deceptively simple, inexhaustibly revealing, and never fully answered. It is the diagnostic heartbeat of this new literacy — the discipline of turning thought into text, and text into truth.

Obligations and Constraints

In December 1999, a software malfunction delayed the launch of NASA's *Mars Climate Orbiter.* The cause was absurdly simple: one team at Lockheed Martin used imperial units, another used metric. No one had enforced a constraint to ensure consistency. The result was catastrophic — a $125 million spacecraft lost because of a missing conversion clause. The engineers had all the intelligence and data they needed, yet without a shared format, the mission drifted into silence. It was not ignorance but indiscipline: an unenforced boundary.

Constraints, in any intelligent system, are what make cooperation possible. They define the perimeter of obligation — the rules that turn effort into alignment. Whether between humans or between human and machine, every collaboration requires structure: inputs that are allowed, tools that are authorised, formats that are mandatory, exclusions that prevent overreach. Without them, even brilliant reasoning degrades into noise. In prompting, these constraints are not stylistic niceties but operational clauses. They turn a language model's statistical tendencies into usable precision.

To understand why constraints matter, consider how ambiguity behaves in generative systems. When an instruction lacks boundaries, the model defaults to its training priors — those vast internal averages of how words have co-occurred across the internet. Ask a model to "summarise this article," and it must infer what "summarise" means: length, tone, inclusion criteria. Ask it instead to "produce a 150-word abstract highlighting methods, findings, and one limitation in bullet form," and its variance collapses. The prompt has become a contract, the constraints enforceable terms. Output stabilises, hallucination declines, and time-to-clarity shortens.

The principle is old, though the context is new. In 1947, at Bell Labs in New Jersey, Claude Shannon formalised information theory by defining *constraints* as the very source of meaning. Signals, he argued, only carry information when they exclude alternatives. The same applies here. A prompt without constraints contains infinite interpretations; only by narrowing scope does it communicate. Each clause — "use dataset X," "respond as a JSON array," "cite at least two sources from after 2020" — is a filter that transforms potential into purpose.

Modern empirical studies support this intuition. In 2023, OpenAI's internal evaluations found that prompts specifying format and exclusion criteria reduced factual errors in generated text by roughly 38% compared with unconstrained prompts (OpenAI Technical Report, July 2023). A similar experiment at the Alan Turing Institute in London measured a 30% reduction in revision cycles for technical documentation when prompts mandated structure and reference type. The conclusion was consistent: constraint saves time because it saves reinterpretation.

Yet constraints do more than protect against drift; they allocate responsibility. In project management, this is called *scope control.*

Every unbounded instruction is an invitation to scope creep — the gradual inflation of expectation without corresponding resources. The same happens with prompts. "Analyse this dataset for insights" is an unlimited liability clause: the model can produce anything from summary statistics to speculative narratives. But "generate a three-point analysis of correlation between variables A and B, using Pearson's r, with interpretive notes under 200 words" confines the obligation. It clarifies what counts as done.

The legal profession has long understood this logic. The phrase "minimum viable contract" refers to the smallest set of clauses that prevents later dispute. In prompting, the equivalent is the *minimum viable constraint*: the minimal specification that ensures interpretive fidelity. Inputs (what data or context may be used). Tools (what computational or reasoning methods are permitted). Formats (what structure results must take). Exclusions (what domains or styles are off-limits). Each element is an insurance policy against misfire. Precision is not pedantry; it is protection.

A practical comparison illustrates the gains. In early 2024, a multinational law firm in London tested generative systems for drafting standard client memos. The unconstrained prompt — "Draft a legal summary of the new data protection rules" — produced 40% unusable text, often including fabricated clauses or non-existent precedents. When reformulated with constraints — "Draft a 500-word legal summary for corporate clients in the UK, limited to GDPR amendments enacted since 2021, written in neutral tone and referencing official ICO guidance" — accuracy rose sharply. Revisions dropped by half. What changed was not the model's intelligence but the human's precision.

This mirrors lessons from engineering and medicine alike. In manufacturing, Toyota's *Andon* system requires explicit thresholds for intervention: when a defect reaches a defined variance, the line stops. Without that rule, workers hesitate, errors accumulate. In clinical research, trial protocols must specify inclusion and exclusion criteria with mathematical exactness. These boundaries are not bureaucracy but ethics — they prevent harm and ensure comparability. The same ethos must govern prompting. Each constraint is a moral commitment to clarity.

Still, there is a counterpoint worth addressing. Constraints, while protective, can sometimes suffocate exploration. In 2017, Google's DeepMind researchers in London experimented with reinforcement learning agents that were *over-constrained* — given so many prohibitions that they learned to do nothing rather than risk error. The lesson applies linguistically: over-specified prompts can trap models into formulaic repetition, robbing them of generative strength. The remedy is proportionality. Constraints should secure the boundaries of intent, not strangle the means of achieving it. A good contract allocates freedom responsibly.

The motif of the "clause" helps to see this balance. Every clause carries both permission and restriction. It defines *how far one may go*. The art lies in drafting language that channels creativity toward valid ends. A prompt that dictates outcome without dictating process invites genuine problem-solving; a prompt that dictates both breeds stagnation. "Solve this equation using any algebraic method" sustains agency. "Solve this equation by performing these five exact steps" denies it. Constraints should shape possibility, not erase it.

Quantitatively, the efficiency of constraint-rich prompting can be measured through iteration cycles — the number of exchanges required to reach acceptable output. At Microsoft Research's Cambridge Lab (2024), studies across 300 professionals showed that adding structural constraints reduced mean iteration count from 3.4 to 1.9 per task. That 44% reduction represented a full hour saved in daily use. In other words, constraint is not merely intellectual hygiene; it is economic leverage. The cost of ambiguity is measurable, and it compounds.

Beyond efficiency lies integrity. Constraints serve as guardrails against hallucination — the model's tendency to generate plausible but false information. When a prompt demands "include only verifiable statistics from named sources," it activates the model's retrieval discipline. When it specifies "state if information cannot be verified," it embeds epistemic humility. The prompt thus becomes self-auditing. This matters not because machines must be humble, but because humans must remain accountable. The constraint enforces honesty at the interface.

There is an instructive historical parallel. In 1895, the mathematician David Hilbert proposed a formal system to axiomatise all of mathematics — a complete, consistent set of constraints. Three decades later, Kurt Gödel proved that such total containment was impossible: any system rich enough to express arithmetic would contain true statements that could not be proven within its own rules. The implication for prompting is subtle but profound. Constraints ensure order, but not omniscience. They create reliability, not perfection. The goal is not absolute containment of meaning but manageable uncertainty.

Constraints, then, operate as both compass and cage. They direct attention, reduce risk, and codify responsibility, but they also reveal where interpretation begins. The professional's task is to calibrate them continuously — tightening when variance threatens quality, loosening when exploration yields value. This calibration is the real craft of prompting. It transforms the writer from supplicant to designer, from consumer of responses to architect of reasoning.

Returning to the image of the *Mars Climate Orbiter*, its demise remains a warning about unspoken assumptions. Units of measurement were the constraint that no one wrote down. A single line — "All data must use SI units" — would have saved the mission. In prompting, such lines are our safeguard against drift. They translate trust into protocol. Without them, we are all launching spacecraft on the faith that meaning will hold its shape.

The question, therefore, is not whether to constrain, but how much. When does specification become straitjacket, and freedom become chaos? Every prompt is a negotiation between certainty and surprise. To master it is to ask, before every exchange: *What boundaries will make this collaboration safe, efficient, and true?* The answer changes with context — but the obligation to ask never does.

Ambiguity, Defaults, and Risk

In March 2018, a self-driving Uber vehicle struck and killed pedestrian Elaine Herzberg in Tempe, Arizona. The car's sensors detected her six seconds before impact but failed to classify her correctly. The system oscillated between "bicycle," "unknown object," and "pedestrian," never assigning a consistent label long enough to trigger braking. The software had no defined response for an ambiguous category, so it defaulted to inaction. The tragedy was not born of malfunction, but of assumption — a failure to define what to do when the world refused to fit a label.

Ambiguity is the quiet architect of failure. In human dialogue, it invites nuance and interpretation; in computational reasoning, it breeds unpredictability. Large language models, like all statistical systems, resolve ambiguity not through understanding but through priors — the patterns of probability encoded in their training data. When words admit multiple meanings, the model must gamble. It guesses what someone *like you* would mean, based on what someone *somewhere* once wrote. That guess may be right often enough to appear intelligent, yet its errors are systematic, not random. The risk lies not in occasional mistake but in predictable misalignment — the way certain kinds of vagueness consistently produce certain kinds of wrongness.

The mechanics of that wrongness are measurable. In 2023, a research team at Stanford University tested how minor linguistic variations altered model outputs. Changing a single adjective — from "safe" to "secure," or "explain briefly" to "summarise concisely" — shifted semantic content distributions by up to 27%, affecting factual density and tone consistency (Stanford NLP Group, July 2023). The finding was not a curiosity; it was a revelation. Words that appear synonymous to humans operate as probabilistic levers to models, each with distinct statistical neighbourhoods. The difference between "convincing" and "accurate" is the difference between rhetoric and truth.

Such sensitivity exposes a deeper reality: ambiguity is not evenly distributed. It clusters around certain linguistic zones — adjectives, comparatives, and implicit assumptions about context. When a professional writes "produce a short report," what constitutes "short"? Fifty words or five hundred? To a model trained on millions of corporate documents, "short" correlates with roughly 350 words. Unless constrained otherwise, that becomes the default. The model is not wrong; it is obedient to its priors. But if the human's mental model differs, friction ensues. The machine's fluency conceals its inference, and the user misreads approximation as alignment.

Defaults, in this sense, are silent participants in every prompt. They are the inherited habits of the data that trained the system. A model trained primarily on English-language text from Western institutions will, by design, treat Western norms as universal. Ask for a "formal letter," and it will default to Anglo-American business etiquette. Request a "balanced argument," and it will approximate balance through median phrasing — equating "both sides" with fairness, even where evidence is asymmetric. These defaults are not moral failings but statistical ones. Yet their consequences can be profound.

In April 2024, the BBC reported a case in which a British student using a language model to draft a research summary on African economic policy received outputs referencing non-existent institutions and misattributed quotes. The prompt — "summarise current African trade initiatives" — was too open. The model defaulted to the most statistically frequent representation of "African trade," heavily skewed toward Western academic discourse from the 1990s. The result was temporally outdated and geographically narrow. When the same task was constrained — "summarise current (post-2020) trade initiatives led by the African Union and ECOWAS, citing verifiable sources" — factual accuracy increased markedly. The correction was not in data, but in definition.

Managing ambiguity, then, is an exercise in surfacing and neutralising defaults. It begins with recognising that no language is neutral. Every term carries hidden coordinates — cultural, temporal, methodological. The role of the professional is not merely to write prompts but to interrogate them: *Which assumptions am I leaving unspoken? Which defaults am I inheriting without consent?* The risk-based mindset replaces hope with method. It treats ambiguity as a quantifiable variable, one that can be mapped, measured, and mitigated.

Risk, in this context, is the probability of misinterpretation multiplied by the impact of its consequence. A vague word in a casual email carries negligible risk; the same word in a compliance report or medical summary can cause material harm. The solution is proportional explicitness. Where stakes are high, precision must tighten. Where stakes are exploratory, ambiguity may be tolerated — even courted — for creative gain. This calibration mirrors aviation's "risk envelope": flight operations accept turbulence in simulation, not in live descent. Prompting, too, must distinguish between experimentation and execution.

A useful precedent lies in the history of engineering language. After the catastrophic *Therac-25* radiation overdoses in Canada (1985–1987), investigators found that ambiguous operator commands — inconsistently parsed by the control software — had caused overdoses exceeding 100 times safe levels. Regulators subsequently enforced unambiguous syntax in medical interfaces: each function required explicit parameter confirmation. The moral was clear. Systems interpret literally, not contextually. Where meaning is not specified, behaviour defaults to internal logic, not human expectation. The same law governs statistical models: they comply with what is said, not what is meant.

There is, however, a nuance worth preserving. Ambiguity is not always an enemy; sometimes it is a lens. In literary translation or exploratory design, deliberate ambiguity invites generative richness. In 2021, Google's Magenta project demonstrated that models given *lightly ambiguous* music composition prompts — such as "melancholy but uncertain tempo" — produced more novel variations than rigidly specified ones. Ambiguity, in these settings, is an engine of divergence. But it must be intentional, bounded by context and purpose. Unacknowledged ambiguity is risk; deliberate ambiguity is creativity. The distinction lies in awareness.

The motif of *the shadow clause* helps to illuminate this. Every instruction contains clauses that are spoken and unspoken. The unspoken ones — the defaults — are the shadows cast by language's probabilities. They can only be managed when made visible. One practical method is adversarial prompting: intentionally writing two near-identical prompts with subtle differences ("explain" versus "justify," "summarise" versus "evaluate") and comparing outputs. The divergence exposes where the model's priors sit. What looks like nuance in phrasing reveals fault lines in interpretation. This technique, used systematically, transforms ambiguity from hazard into diagnostic tool.

Such testing reflects a shift from reactive correction to proactive governance. Instead of waiting for errors, professionals can map their prompt's risk surface before deployment. In 2024, researchers at Oxford's Internet Institute proposed a framework for "linguistic risk analysis," ranking prompt ambiguity along three axes: lexical vagueness (word-level uncertainty), structural ambiguity (multi-clause dependency), and contextual drift (assumed but unstated frames). Early experiments in journalism and legal drafting showed that identifying high-risk zones reduced revision effort by a third. Risk awareness, not word count, proved the decisive factor.

The trade-off, however, remains perennial. Precision consumes time; ambiguity buys speed. The question becomes: *How much risk can I afford per word?* In low-stakes creative drafting, the answer may be generous. In regulatory reporting or code generation, it is near zero. The mature practitioner learns to budget ambiguity the way an investor budgets volatility — allocating it where returns justify exposure. This is the strategic heart of prompting: not control for its own sake, but control in proportion to consequence.

Defaults also evolve. As models retrain on newer data, yesterday's priors become obsolete. What once seemed neutral — like "gendered pronouns" or "formal tone" — shifts as cultural norms shift. The responsible user maintains situational awareness, testing old prompts against new behaviours. Ambiguity that once yielded harmless variance may, under new priors, yield bias or factual distortion. The contract metaphor endures: clauses must be reviewed as conditions change. Trust is not a one-time signature but an ongoing audit.

The central risk is complacency. Because models produce language that *sounds* certain, users mistake fluency for fidelity. The danger is not chaos but coherence — the illusion that ambiguity has been resolved simply because it has been replaced by words. A confident wrong answer is harder to detect than a hesitant one. Calibration prompts — "State your confidence level" or "List uncertainties in your reasoning" — expose that illusion. They return ambiguity to visibility, which is where it belongs.

Ambiguity, defaults, and risk form the unspoken triangle beneath every intelligent dialogue. They determine whether language becomes bridge or trap. The task, for any serious practitioner, is to read prompts as one reads contracts — searching not only for what is written, but for what is implied. The defaults will always be there, waiting in the margins, ready to act as stand-ins for our neglected clarity.

The open question, therefore, is this: when you next issue an instruction — to a colleague, a system, or a self — which part of its meaning have you left to chance?

Verification and Remedies

On 4 June 1996 at Kourou, French Guiana, Ariane 5 Flight 501 veered from its trajectory and self-destructed thirty-seven seconds after launch. The European Space Agency's inquiry found that a 64-bit floating-point number was converted into a 16-bit integer, overflowed, and crashed the inertial reference system; the software, reused from Ariane 4, had not been verified against Ariane 5's higher horizontal velocity (ESA Inquiry Board, 1996). No acceptance test modelled that new regime. No contingency handled the exception. The rocket obeyed the code; the code had never been forced to prove itself. Build the gate first, always.

That failure illustrates the missing half of any contract: enforcement. Instruction without verification is ceremony. We may state purpose, scope and exclusions with elegance, yet if we do not couple deliverables to checks and remedies, we rely on hope rather than control. Verification prompts and acceptance tests are the gates through which outputs must pass. They are simple in spirit and strict in effect: *Show me what you did; prove that it meets the terms; say what happens if it does not.* When those gates are absent, defaults decide. When they are present, language becomes measurable.

The logic is visible in everyday work. Show: have the system expose its steps or sources. Name: call the check an acceptance test rather than a suggestion. Explain: this forces alignment between instruction and evidence. Implication: once a test exists, anyone can run it, and disputes shrink. In prompting practice, a verification prompt might demand evidence ("Cite the two sources you used and quote them for each claim") or a computation trace ("List the intermediate calculations and check totals sum to 100%"). The behaviour is concrete. The cost is small. The effect is cumulative.

Where do red-team loops fit? They are pre-emptive gates — engineered attempts to break promises before the world does. In security, this is routine: teams simulate attackers to expose weak assumptions. In intelligent systems, a red-team loop challenges the instruction itself. Show: create adversarial cases, not happy-path examples. Name: call them failure probes. Explain: they test the *language* of the contract as much as the model's behaviour. Implication: once you have a library of probes, each new deliverable must face them. Errors become repeatable and, therefore, fixable.

The stakes become clear when money moves faster than judgement. On 1 August 2012 at the New York Stock Exchange, Knight Capital Group deployed new trading software without fully testing a dormant code path; within forty-five minutes, it had executed a storm of unintended orders and lost $440 million. The U.S. Securities and Exchange Commission's report traced the catastrophe to missing deployment checks and the absence of a kill-switch (SEC, 2013). The observable behaviours — no dry run in a production-like environment, no acceptance criteria for order volume, no automated rollback — map directly onto our motif. The gates were open; nothing stood between a latent defect and the market.

Contrast that with Netflix's long-running practice of chaos engineering. Beginning in 2011 in Los Gatos, California, engineers released "Chaos Monkey" to terminate random instances in production during business hours (Netflix Tech Blog, 2011). Show: the system proves resilience by surviving deliberate failure. Name: this is an acceptance test for availability at runtime, not a theory. Explain: by making faults routine, they prevent faults from being catastrophic. Implication: a culture that tests under stress develops remedies in advance — circuit breakers, retries, bulkheads — rather than inventing them under duress. The gate here is continuous and kinetic: production itself becomes the test harness.

What does this mean for language with machines? It means we must weld checks to output. A deliverable that "looks right" is a liability if it cannot *demonstrate* rightness. In practice, a verification prompt encodes an acceptance test the way a procurement contract encodes a warranty. "Return a JSON array of three policy risks; include one verifiable statistic per risk with its source; if any source is missing or older than 2020, state 'Insufficient evidence' and stop." The check and the remedy travel with the request. Hallucination has nowhere to hide because verifying it is part of the work, not an afterthought.

This approach aligns with formal guidance. The U.S. National Institute of Standards and Technology's *AI Risk Management Framework* (January 2023) stresses measurable criteria for system behaviour and documentation of evaluation methods (NIST, 2023). Name the test. Tie it to a property. Log the result. A verification prompt operationalises that ethos at the smallest unit of work: the instruction. It turns airy hopes into binary questions, and binary questions into accountable outcomes.

Of course, red-teaming and acceptance tests are not free. They cost time, and in settings where responsiveness is itself a service, every minute matters. A credible counter-example appears in emergency product rollouts. During the first wave of COVID-19, teams at Johns Hopkins University published a global dashboard (March 2020) and improved it in public. Extensive pre-release testing would have delayed life-saving visibility; the remedy was asymmetric: ship early with narrow claims and instrument the system for rapid correction. The gate moved downstream into observability and staged updates. The reconciliation is instructive. Verification is compulsory, but its locus can shift: pre-release for safety-critical changes; post-release with guardrails for informational tools; continuous for resilience.

An acceptance test is only as strong as its specificity. Saying "ensure quality" is useless. Saying "reject if any numerical claim lacks a cited source" is a decision. Saying "flag any proper noun not found in a named knowledge base" is a behaviour. The more a test describes an observable event, the less it depends on taste. This is why coupling language to measurement matters. Words do not verify themselves. They must point to a trace, a reference, a count, a threshold. When we ask for "balanced coverage," we should demand a visible distribution — for example, "allocate approximately one-third of the summary to each perspective, and state that allocation as percentages." The gate becomes countable.

Red-team loops thrive on inversion. If a prompt says "Use only post-2020 sources," the red-team asks for edge cases: sources published online in December 2019 but updated in 2021; preprints; pages with ambiguous metadata. Show: the system's behaviour under ambiguous constraints. Name: boundary probes. Explain: boundaries are where defaults sneak back in. Implication: by forcing articulation of "what counts," we strengthen the contract. The discipline is portable. In legal drafting, scenario tests are common; in software, fuzzing attacks inputs with randomness. In prompting, adversarial paraphrases ("justify" versus "explain," "critique" versus "summarise") expose semantic fault lines before clients do.

There is a second-order benefit. Verification prompts create *witness marks* — traces that reveal tampering or inconsistency. Horologists scribe witness marks inside antique clocks to show how gears once aligned; inspectors can later see what changed. In our craft, a verification step leaves a trail: a versioned test, a timestamped citation, a stated uncertainty. When outputs drift, we do not argue about impressions; we follow the marks. This saves time because it reduces debate. It builds trust because it admits fallibility without drama.

Consider the United Kingdom's Government Digital Service Standard, which since 2019 requires services to "test end-to-end" and publish performance metrics on the GOV.UK Performance Platform. Show: the public can see latency, completion rates, and user satisfaction. Name: these are acceptance criteria at service scale. Explain: measurement externalises quality; it stops being an internal boast. Implication: when people know the gate is public, effort shifts towards meeting it rather than narrating around it. A similar spirit guides the U.S. Food and Drug Administration's software validation guidance for medical devices: testing must be traceable to requirements and documented (FDA, updated guidance 2002). The precise statutes differ, but the theme holds: tie language to evidence; keep the evidence.

What about false alarms? Aggressive red-teaming can swamp teams with spurious failures. This is not a reason to relax gates; it is a reason to calibrate them. Triage proves vital. Assign severity levels before testing begins. Decide up front which failures block release and which prompt a warning. This is a behavioural choice, not a slogan. Teams that pre-commit avoid retrofitting rules to decisions they have already made, a trap that corrodes credibility. The acceptance gate is a place for decisions stated in advance.

When working with language models, acceptance tests often begin with the mundane. Ask the system to restate the instruction in its own words. Have it list the tests it believes it must pass. It sounds almost childish, yet the behaviour surfaces misinterpretation with startling efficiency. If the restatement misses a clause, stop and correct. If the listed tests omit a requirement, add it and repeat. The metric here is simple: count how many clarifying turns are needed before the model can name the gate. A falling count over similar tasks signals learning and better prompts.

Remedies must be as explicit as tests. If a deliverable fails a gate, what happens? In software, continuous integration systems reject the build; developers cannot merge until tests pass. In language work, we need the same bluntness. If any citation cannot be retrieved, label the answer *provisional* and isolate the unverified claims. If a calculation fails to reconcile, halt with an error message rather than fabricating consistency. The choice to stop is itself a remedy. It converts silent failure into visible friction.

Verification does more than block defects; it disciplines style. When a prompt requires a specific format — a schema, an audit table, an uncertainty section — it pushes the model away from persuasive but empty fluency. This has measurable impact. In internal evaluations reported by Google's Responsible AI group (2022), requiring a "Known Unknowns" section reduced unsupported assertions in technical summaries and increased citation rates. Name the behaviour you want; make it non-optional. The gate reshapes the path.

We should also be honest about context. In domains saturated with tacit knowledge — literary criticism, exploratory design — hard acceptance tests can feel stifling. Here, we can shift the gates from *what to say* to *how to show work*. Ask for competing hypotheses. Ask for explicit hedges. Ask for a final paragraph that lists the strongest counterargument and the author's best reply. The test becomes epistemic rather than factual. It creates a remedy for overconfidence rather than a filter for arithmetic. You still build the gate; you place it differently.

Our motif returns. A gate separates promise from delivery. It is not an ornament; it is a load-bearing structure. When professionals say "we test," what they often mean is "we sample." Sampling finds defects by luck. Gates find defects by design. That distinction is the difference between Ariane 5's catastrophic assumption and Netflix's routine resilience, between Knight Capital's ruin and a trading platform that refuses to execute orders when anomaly thresholds trip.

There remains a decision that cannot be outsourced: where to set the gate. Too low, and defects flood through. Too high, and nothing ships. The discipline taught here cannot answer that for you; it gives you a way to decide. What is the worst plausible failure? How visible will it be? What remedy would you accept if it occurred? Until you can name those, you have not finished writing the contract. The next time an output "looks fine," ask a harder question: which gate did it pass, and which gate did you forget to build?

Chapter 2
Minds in the Loop

In 1953, at the Cavendish Laboratory in Cambridge, James Watson and Francis Crick walked into the Eagle pub and announced they had "found the secret of life." They were referring, of course, to the double-helix structure of DNA — a revelation not born of a single flash of insight, but of hundreds of iterative dialogues: between theory and experiment, data and deduction, one hypothesis after another tested and revised. Each sketch on the lab bench, each recalibration of X-ray data from Rosalind Franklin's photographs, was part of a recursive loop — a conversation with reality itself. It was the rhythm of discovery: propose, test, observe, adjust. The dialogue *was* the experiment.

Every interaction with an intelligent system now echoes that rhythm. The prompt is the hypothesis, the model's output the observation, the revision the next hypothesis. What separates the amateur from the master is not access to better tools but adherence to this experimental cadence. Those who treat prompting as dialogue, not dictation, build systems that learn. Those who treat it as a one-shot transaction remain at the mercy of chance. Minds in the loop — human and machine alike — evolve through iteration, not declaration.

This chapter is about building that iterative intelligence. It argues that prompting is not the art of command, but the craft of controlled feedback. Each exchange is an experiment: a test of clarity, of framing, of the model's capacity to mirror intent. Every response is a dataset, every correction a recalibration. Over time, a skilled practitioner learns to log patterns, compare variants, and extract principles. Prompting thus becomes a form of experimental design — with words as instruments and attention as currency.

The modern paradox is that while models scale exponentially, attention does not. Human cognition remains bounded by fatigue, distraction, and diminishing returns. Attention, as Herbert Simon observed in 1971, "consumes information; it does not produce it." The challenge is no longer how much intelligence we can access, but how judiciously we can direct our attention through it. Minds in the loop must therefore learn to budget focus: to decide when precision is worth the cost, and when approximation suffices. The scarce resource is not data, nor even compute, but concentration.

To manage that scarcity, effective workflows distribute precision strategically. Professionals who work fluently with generative systems already practise forms of *staged prompting* — the decomposition of complex reasoning into discrete, manageable steps. A researcher begins with broad exploration, narrows with diagnostic queries, and then refines with verification. A designer drafts, critiques, and re-briefs. A data analyst asks for structured outputs first, interpretations later. Each stage shields attention from cognitive overload, preserving it for judgment rather than reconstruction. The loop tightens, and quality rises not through more effort but through better sequencing.

This method echoes the history of disciplined inquiry. The philosopher Francis Bacon, in *Novum Organum* (1620), warned that intellect untested by experiment "glides to the general and rests there." His proposed remedy was iterative empiricism: to move in loops of hypothesis and verification, never mistaking fluency for truth. The same corrective applies to our interaction with machines. Fluent systems tempt us to accept their first replies as finished thought. But fluency is only form; reliability is achieved through iteration. Each turn in the dialogue must test the assumptions embedded in the last. The loop replaces faith with method.

When practitioners adopt this cadence, reliability compounds. Each prompt becomes not just a request but a data point in a personal experiment. By comparing a control prompt and its variant — adjusting phrasing, scope, or constraints — one can observe shifts in accuracy and tone. Patterns emerge: which instructions tighten reasoning, which loosen it. Over time, intuition matures into knowledge. The practice resembles experimental psychology more than programming: design the conditions, vary one factor, record the outcome, revise the hypothesis. The difference is that the laboratory is now linguistic.

Yet the human factor remains decisive. The loop works only if the human stays present, not as supervisor but as collaborator. A system can iterate, but it cannot *care*. It lacks the evaluative compass that distinguishes novelty from nonsense. That compass is judgment — an asset that must be rationed. When attention thins, evaluation falters, and errors pass unchallenged. Hence the importance of structured delegation: automate routine phrasing, predefine output schemas, and batch low-stakes queries, so that scarce human discernment can be reserved for interpretation and ethical scrutiny. The goal is not to eliminate effort but to concentrate it where it yields insight.

Error, too, must be reclassified. In a looped dialogue, mistakes are not failures but signals — data about the boundary of understanding. The recurring types of failure are surprisingly stable: misread intent, missing constraint, lexical ambiguity, and domain mismatch. Each corresponds to a distinct breakdown in the prompt-contract established earlier. Skilled users learn to diagnose them on sight. A misread intent shows up in tone: the model answers *a* question, just not *the* question. A missing constraint leads to overreach — too much information, too little focus. Ambiguity produces stylistic or factual drift. Domain mismatch reveals itself when the model reasons confidently outside its training competence. The triage is linguistic, not technical: fix the prompt, not the prose.

The motif of triage matters. In medicine, triage is not about perfection but priority — identifying what must be treated first to prevent systemic failure. Prompt triage follows the same logic. When an interaction derails, the fastest path to recovery is to classify the fault, isolate the cause, and reissue a targeted query. This mental taxonomy prevents wasted cycles. It turns confusion into clarity and error into education. Every correction strengthens the model's alignment with the user's reasoning pattern. The loop, once painful, becomes reflexive.

To close that loop, feedback must teach, not merely correct. A blunt rejection — "That's wrong" — provides no information. A constructive prompt does. "That's wrong because it misclassified the source; re-examine it with attention to publication date." Exemplars, rationales, and counterexamples train not just the current output but the future state of the system. When tools support memory, feedback can even persist — a private curriculum of refinement. When they do not, disciplined users create their own logs: a record of what worked, why it worked, and where it failed. Over time, such archives become the scaffolding of expertise.

The most productive partnerships between human and machine therefore resemble apprenticeship. The model is not a servant to command, but a student to instruct — one that learns quickly but forgets without reinforcement. Each prompt becomes a lesson; each verification a tutorial. The relationship matures through reciprocity: the human refines their articulation, the model refines its approximation of meaning. Together they form a composite intelligence, bounded yet cumulative.

But there is also danger here. Loops can harden into routines, and routines can blind. If iteration becomes mechanical, learning halts. The professional must preserve a spirit of curiosity within the method — to see each exchange as an opportunity for surprise, not merely optimisation. Iteration should stabilise accuracy, not sterilise thought. The loop must remain alive.

Minds in the Loop is therefore a manifesto for disciplined curiosity. It invites readers to treat dialogue not as transaction but as transformation. To experiment, to observe, to revise — not once, but continually. To recognise that the most advanced systems still rely on the oldest scientific truth: that knowledge grows by testing what one believes to be true. The reader will learn not how to automate thought, but how to shape it through feedback. The reward is not speed alone, but reliability — a new literacy of interaction where both human and machine learn, together, to think in loops.

The Dialogue as Experiment

In January 1961, at the Massachusetts Institute of Technology, a psychologist named J.C.R. Licklider published a memorandum titled *Man-Computer Symbiosis.* He predicted that human thought and machine processing would one day form a "cooperative interaction"

— a conversation rather than a command. His contemporaries viewed it as fanciful: computers were lumbering machines fed by punch cards, not partners in reasoning. Yet Licklider's wager was precise. The future of intelligence, he argued, would depend not on faster hardware but on iterative dialogue — cycles of hypothesis, response, and refinement between human and system. More than sixty years later, his memo reads less like prophecy than like field notes from the world we now inhabit.

Every exchange with an intelligent model is an experiment in miniature. The prompt is the hypothesis, the model's output the observation, and the revision the next hypothesis. The variable under test is language itself. When phrasing changes, results shift; when conditions tighten, reliability rises. The aim is not to find the perfect prompt but to cultivate an experimental cadence — a steady rhythm of testing and improvement that compounds insight over time. Fluency is seductive, but it is iteration that builds understanding.

The motif of the *loop* defines this practice. Each return to the model re-enters the loop: hypothesis → test → observation → revision. When logged with discipline, these loops accumulate into data — a private record of reasoning patterns, linguistic sensitivities, and model behaviour. This record is not a transcript of conversations; it is a research diary. It shows what language does, not merely what it says.

The strength of this approach lies in its lineage. Consider the work of the physicist Michael Faraday, whose notebooks between 1820 and 1862 remain masterpieces of experimental thought. Each entry followed a cadence — propose a principle, perform a test, record the deviation, adjust the model. Faraday did not "believe" his hypotheses; he interrogated them. His marginalia are dense with verbs: *observe, compare, alter, repeat.* The pattern mirrors modern prompt engineering. Those who treat dialogue as data replicate Faraday's discipline, only their instruments are linguistic rather than electrical.

A contrasting case illuminates the danger of one-shot thinking. In 2019, researchers at OpenAI conducted controlled evaluations of large language models to test factual consistency. They found that unrefined prompts achieved factual accuracy scores of around 40–50%, while carefully iterated versions — structured through a sequence of clarifying sub-prompts — reached over 80% (OpenAI Technical Report, 2019). The improvement did not come from more information, but from method: each iteration acted as an experiment, exposing hidden assumptions and guiding the model toward coherence. Without feedback loops, even the most advanced systems revert to statistical surface-play.

Iteration is not indulgence; it is insurance. Every untested prompt is a gamble on unexamined priors. A single round of questioning might appear efficient, but efficiency without validation is waste. The iterative method replaces hope with measurement. It begins modestly: vary one parameter, log the difference, note the outcome. The small discipline of comparison is what transforms prompting from intuition to science.

In practice, control and variant prompts perform the role of laboratory conditions. The control maintains baseline phrasing; the variant isolates a change — a new verb, a tighter constraint, an altered audience. The difference between outputs is evidence. When recorded systematically, such experiments reveal the behavioural contour of a model: its biases toward verbosity, its thresholds of ambiguity, its response to hierarchy or tone. Over time, the practitioner builds not superstition ("this wording works") but empiricism ("this wording produces this effect, under these conditions").

This method scales naturally into domains that already speak the language of experiment. In product design, A/B testing became a discipline precisely because intuition proved unreliable. The same principle applies here. The prompt is the design; the output is the user response. Reliability improves not through genius but through iteration. To think experimentally is to make peace with correction. Each exchange teaches you how to ask better questions, and each revision becomes a hypothesis tested against reality.

There are limits. Experiments require stability, but models change. Updates to training data or architectures can alter behaviour overnight, erasing the reliability painstakingly earned. This instability recalls the experience of early pharmacologists in the 1930s, who discovered that batch variability in biological reagents rendered some assays meaningless. Their remedy was calibration: to run control samples alongside every new batch. The same discipline applies to prompting. When a model updates, retest known prompts against known benchmarks before resuming critical work. Verification, not nostalgia, guards against drift.

The experimental stance also carries a psychological demand: tolerance for ambiguity. Many professionals are trained for decisiveness, not exploration. They want closure, not probability. Yet dialogue with probabilistic systems resists closure. It rewards those who frame uncertainty as an ally. Each ambiguous response is an opportunity to discover how the model generalises, where it overfits, and which cues mislead it. Treating uncertainty as data converts frustration into insight. The most adept practitioners are less judges than ethnographers: they study the model's behaviour as one might study a culture — through observation, comparison, and disciplined curiosity.

A quiet motif threads through this practice: *temperature*. In machine learning, "temperature" controls randomness in generation. High values produce diversity; low values yield predictability. But temperature is also a metaphor for tone — the heat of experimentation itself. If one's dialogue runs perpetually cold, fixed in rigid procedure, discovery cools. If it burns too hot, chaos returns. The craft lies in modulation: cool enough to measure, warm enough to explore. This balance between curiosity and control defines mastery.

Real-world laboratories of dialogue already exist. At DeepMind's AlphaCode project (London, 2022), engineers improved algorithmic code synthesis by prompting models with multiple near-identical problem statements and ranking their solutions statistically. The winning prompt was not guessed; it was measured. Across 10,000 programming tasks, success rates improved when prompts were treated as experimental variables rather than static instructions (DeepMind Research Blog, 2022). The principle extends far beyond code. In any domain where reasoning meets language — law, policy, research — prompt variation functions as hypothesis testing, a way to explore cognitive space efficiently.

A credible counterpoint comes from creative writing, where over-analysis can suffocate imagination. The poet cannot A/B test a metaphor without killing it. Yet even here, an experimental mindset need not sterilise intuition. Iteration can serve inspiration rather than inhibition. Writers from Virginia Woolf to Italo Calvino revised through dialogue — not with machines, but with themselves — treating each draft as an experiment in tone and perspective. What changes is not the art but the awareness of process. Iteration is simply reflection with evidence.

Logging outcomes turns iteration into memory. A notebook, a spreadsheet, a version history — these are not bureaucratic relics but instruments of thought. They externalise cognition, freeing the mind to think about *differences* rather than recollecting details. The metric need not be complex: accuracy, conciseness, consistency. The act of logging itself sharpens attention. As the philosopher Donald Schön wrote in *The Reflective Practitioner* (1983), professionals become expert by reflecting on their experiments in action. Dialogue, when logged, becomes such reflection — a mirror held up to method.

When executed with care, the experimental cadence compounds value. Small refinements accumulate. Error rates fall. Outputs converge toward dependable standards. The practitioner's intuition matures from anecdote to anticipation. It is the same compounding observed in engineering and medicine: repetition plus feedback yields expertise. The paradox is that reliability, far from stifling creativity, liberates it. Once you trust the process, you are free to explore its edges.

Still, a tension endures. Experiment demands both patience and humility — virtues that modern attention rarely rewards. The temptation is always to rush, to treat dialogue as transaction rather than investigation. Yet the cost of haste is hidden in rework: the time lost correcting what a controlled test could have prevented. The diagnostic question remains: are you conversing to finish, or conversing to learn? The latter is slower but surer. The former feels efficient but builds nothing that lasts.

The dialogue-as-experiment is not a metaphor; it is a method. It is how minds, human and artificial, learn together. To think experimentally is to honour the oldest principle of progress: that truth is iterative, that knowledge matures through correction, and that clarity is earned one prompt at a time. The next time you type an instruction and wait for an answer, ask yourself what Licklider asked of his imagined symbiosis in 1961: not "What can the machine do for me?" but "What can we discover together if I treat this exchange as an experiment?"

Human Attention as Scarce Resource

In March 1973, at the Stanford University psychology department, Daniel Kahneman and Amos Tversky presented a series of papers that would later redefine behavioural economics. One of them, *Attention and Effort*, offered a deceptively simple premise: attention is not infinite. It is a finite, consumable resource — as measurable as oxygen in a tank. Every act of concentration depletes it; every demand on it incurs a cost. Kahneman's experiments quantified that cost in milliseconds and recall errors. But the principle transcends the lab: when attention is overspent, judgment falters.

Half a century later, that same economy governs our exchanges with intelligent systems. The cognitive budget of a professional or researcher is no longer consumed by reading reports or running calculations; it is consumed by *managing interactions*. The prompt has replaced the memo, the chat interface the meeting room. Yet the same biological constraint persists: there are only so many high-quality decisions one mind can make in a day. The problem is not that we lack tools, but that we scatter attention too widely across them. The result is what cognitive scientists now call "decision fatigue" — the silent tax on performance that accumulates with every unnecessary choice.

The question, then, is not how to extract more work from attention, but how to spend it where it pays. Attention is not a reservoir to hoard but a currency to allocate. The most capable users of AI systems are not those who ask the most, but those who design workflows that protect their mental economy. They treat attention as budget, precision as investment, and prompting as portfolio management. Every word is a trade-off between depth and depletion.

The structure of an effective workflow mirrors the design of good architecture: load-bearing where necessary, lightweight elsewhere. Consider DeepMind's AlphaFold team in London (2021). Faced with millions of protein sequences, researchers had to decide which regions of the sequence to model with full computational rigour and which to approximate. The choice was dictated not by ambition but by attention. They developed batching systems to run lower-confidence sequences automatically and reserve manual review for edge cases. Accuracy rose, time fell, and cognitive exhaustion — once the unspoken bottleneck — eased. The principle applies beyond science. Precision is expensive; use it where stakes justify the spend.

In language work, precision costs tokens, review cycles, and patience. Each unnecessary clarification prompt or redundant verification is a withdrawal from the cognitive bank. Professionals who thrive in human–machine dialogue learn to stage their engagement: start wide, filter fast, focus deep. The technique known as *progressive disclosure* — first formalised in software usability research by Jakob Nielsen (1993) — remains powerful here. Rather than overwhelm the model with all context at once, or the human with all output at once, information is revealed incrementally. The first pass sketches the landscape; subsequent prompts illuminate details. The rhythm mirrors the scientific method: coarse measurement, refined measurement, final confirmation. Each stage conserves mental bandwidth by postponing complexity until it becomes relevant.

The motif of *the lens* captures this elegantly. A wide lens captures possibility; a narrow lens captures precision. Skilled practitioners learn to switch lenses with purpose. The initial wide lens establishes context — asking the model for summaries, comparisons, or categories. Once key dimensions emerge, the lens narrows: detailed exploration, source verification, numerical alignment. The final lens, the microscope, inspects anomalies. This progression preserves attention for interpretation rather than correction. When done well, it resembles triage in emergency medicine: identify the critical few, defer the rest.

Batching is the operational twin of staged prompting. Rather than issue a dozen ad-hoc queries, a practitioner groups similar tasks — for example, requesting parallel analyses under a shared schema — to reduce cognitive switching. The metric is time-to-clarity per cognitive unit. In a 2022 study by Microsoft Research, analysts who batched similar natural-language queries reduced average task completion time by 23% while improving self-rated understanding of results. The finding was unsurprising to anyone trained in industrial design or aviation: context switching burns attention. Grouping stabilises it. The same rule applies to prompting.

There is an old lesson from air traffic control that still resonates. In 2002, after a mid-air collision over Überlingen, Germany, investigators found that excessive cognitive load — too many simultaneous monitoring tasks — had led a single controller to overlook a critical radar warning. The subsequent human factors report (BFU, 2004) reshaped international standards: redistribute attention; automate detection; preserve judgment for intervention. The same three imperatives now apply to digital workflows. Automation should absorb pattern recognition; humans should adjudicate ambiguity. Every prompt that removes trivial verification from a person's head and embeds it in a system is a gain in safety and quality.

Yet there is a counterpoint worth examining. Over-automation can breed complacency. When systems absorb too much cognitive labour, human attention atrophies. The 2010 Deepwater Horizon disaster inquiry noted this paradox: automated alarms were so frequent and so often false that crews tuned them out. Attention was not overused but misused — scattered across noise rather than conserved for signal. The reconciliation lies in *meaningful load*: attention should be taxed only where its judgment adds value. Every alert, every output, every interaction must justify its cost in focus.

The psychology of this economy is ancient. The medieval monastic practice of *lectio divina* — slow, deliberate reading of sacred texts — rested on the belief that attention purified understanding. The monks' rituals of pacing and silence were not aesthetic; they were ergonomic. They engineered an environment where focus could endure. The modern professional faces the same challenge without the cloister: to build conditions where attention can sustain precision. The tools are different, the principle identical.

Progressive prompting can function as such a discipline. Instead of confronting an ocean of possibility, one works through a sequence of gates. Each prompt narrows uncertainty; each response defines the next question. The human remains inside the loop, not as labourer but as arbiter. Judgment is exercised sparingly but decisively. This structure prevents quality regressions — the gradual drift toward superficiality that occurs when tasks are fragmented and attention dispersed. A well-designed prompt chain acts like a workflow checklist: it embeds cognitive sequence into language.

A historical analogue can be seen in the checklists developed by surgeon Atul Gawande and colleagues at the World Health Organization in 2008. They found that introducing structured preoperative and postoperative questions — only nineteen items long — reduced surgical mortality by nearly one third (WHO Safe Surgery Study, 2009). The mechanism was not information but focus. The checklist reallocated scarce attention to the most consequential points of failure. The same logic governs high-stakes prompting: a simple structure catches what fatigue would miss.

Attention, however, is not only individual but collective. In collaborative projects involving multiple analysts or writers, shared mental bandwidth becomes a coordination problem. If one member refines prompts while another verifies sources, efficiency rises — but only if communication friction stays low. Clear role delineation and shared templates convert attention from isolated effort to pooled intelligence. The analogy to ensemble performance in music is apt: each player manages limited focus, yet the composition demands synchrony. One dissonant entry dissipates the ensemble's energy.

A credible counterexample to the attention-as-budget model comes from the world of creative improvisation. Jazz musicians and performance artists often report entering *flow* states in which attention feels boundless. But research by psychologist Mihaly Csikszentmihalyi (1990) revealed that such flow arises only within structured boundaries — clear goals, immediate feedback, and manageable challenge. Constraint, paradoxically, is what frees attention from fragmentation. In human–machine collaboration, constraint functions similarly. Structure does not stifle; it focuses.

The motif of *the ledger* offers a closing reflection. Attention leaves traces — the hours spent, the revisions made, the fatigue that follows. Like a financial ledger, it reveals patterns of waste and investment. Professionals who keep a simple record of where their attention goes — which prompts required the most clarification, which stages produced the most rework — gain visibility into their cognitive expenditure. From this evidence they can redesign their workflows. The act of measurement itself improves allocation, just as budgeting improves spending.

The unresolved question, however, remains: how much precision is worth the cost? When does vigilance become waste, and automation become risk? The line cannot be drawn by rule. It must be judged, case by case, through reflection. Attention is the last non-scalable resource in a scalable world. Every word we type either spends it or saves it. The art of prompting — and perhaps the art of thinking — lies in knowing the difference.

Error Taxonomy and Recovery

In April 2010, a team of analysts at the Icelandic Meteorological Office misclassified a plume of volcanic ash from Eyjafjallajökull as low-density vapour. Within hours, their model had propagated that assumption across airspace forecasts, triggering flight cancellations across Northern Europe. Over 100,000 flights were grounded and airlines lost an estimated £1.1 billion over the following week (Eurocontrol Report, 2010). The error was not computational. It was linguistic. The input description — *"visible plume with intermittent emissions"* — was read by the forecasting model as weak activity. Human operators had meant *unsteady but severe*. One word misread, thousands of decisions derailed.

Language errors scale faster than numerical ones. Where a spreadsheet error distorts a column, a mis-specified prompt distorts a system. The same logic applies to intelligent models. Each exchange carries an implicit contract of meaning. When that contract breaks, failures fall into patterns. Misread intent, missing constraint, ambiguity, and domain mismatch are not abstract categories; they are the fingerprints of misunderstanding. Classifying them is the first act of recovery — the moment one stops rewriting prose and starts repairing reasoning.

The motif of *triage* helps frame this process. In medicine, triage separates what must be treated immediately from what can wait. In prompting, triage distinguishes between an error of expression and an error of structure. The former is surface-level — a misplaced word, an unclear scope. The latter is systemic — an assumption misaligned with the model's priors or the domain's boundaries. Diagnosis precedes cure. Without it, correction risks deepening confusion.

The first and most common category is **misread intent**. It occurs when the model infers purpose incorrectly because the prompt's verbs or framing cues lead it astray. A 2022 study by Anthropic researchers found that changing a single directive verb — "summarise" to "analyse" — shifted output structure by over 30%, even when all other parameters were held constant. The behaviour was consistent: models overfit to command words, treating them as dominant signals of intent. The visible symptom is tone or structure mismatch — responses that are polished but directionless. The repair pattern is simple but rigorous: restate the prompt as a goal, not a gesture. Instead of *"Write an overview of X"*, use *"Produce a 200-word summary explaining causes and consequences of X, distinguishing data from commentary."* The test of correction is not satisfaction but repeatability: if the model can restate the instruction in its own words without drift, intent has been captured.

The second failure class is **missing constraint** — the silent inflation of scope. The model fills gaps generously; omission invites expansion. In 2021, researchers at OpenAI found that unconstrained prompts increased average token output by 70% compared to those specifying length, tone, or exclusion criteria. More text does not mean more content; it means more entropy. Missing constraints are expensive because they waste both human and computational attention. The diagnostic probe is quantitative: measure verbosity or topic breadth across repeated runs. If variance exceeds tolerance, the constraint is incomplete. Repair requires explicit framing of limits. Constraints are not restrictions but coordinates. They define where the conversation begins and ends, sparing the user from policing digression manually.

The third pattern, **ambiguity**, is subtler. It lives in words that humans understand socially but models interpret statistically. Adjectives are the main culprits — *"simple"*, *"balanced"*, *"innovative"*. Each hides a spectrum of meaning. The Oxford Internet Institute's 2024 analysis of AI-assisted journalism found that prompts containing two or more adjectives of judgment ("persuasive", "strong", "insightful") produced factual errors 40% more often than neutral phrasing. The reason is mechanical: evaluative adjectives pull the model toward stylistic imitation rather than evidential reasoning. The repair is disambiguation by demonstration. Replace adjectives with measurable targets — *"Include three arguments with one counterpoint each"* achieves what *"balanced analysis"* only implies.

Domain mismatch is the final, and often most dangerous, category. It occurs when the model operates outside the boundaries of its trained competence. In 2023, an American law firm (Mata v. Avianca) submitted a legal brief drafted with a language model that cited six non-existent court cases. The prompt — *"Provide supporting precedents for this claim"* — presumed a legal research capability the model did not possess. The issue was not deceit but domain drift: a statistical model simulating authority within an epistemic space it could not verify. The visible symptom is confidence without evidence. The diagnostic probe is provenance testing — ask the system to cite sources or specify data provenance. When it cannot, the mismatch is confirmed. The remedy is rerouting, not refinement: delegate to a verified corpus or tool specialised for that domain.

Yet error is rarely singular. Most failures blend classes. A missing constraint invites ambiguity; misread intent amplifies domain mismatch. Effective triage, therefore, proceeds hierarchically. Begin with intent — *what was I trying to achieve?* Then scope — *what did I fail to bound?* Then language — *which terms allowed multiple readings?* Finally, domain — *does the system know enough to answer?* This sequence mirrors incident analysis in engineering, where investigators first check specifications before instruments. The discipline is not punitive; it is preventative.

Two historical examples illuminate how structured recovery transforms failure into learning. The first comes from the NASA Mars Climate Orbiter (1999). The spacecraft was lost because one engineering team used imperial units while another used metric. The post-mortem identified the error not as numerical but communicative: "a failure to specify interface constraints." The remedy was institutional — enforce unit verification at every cross-team boundary. The second comes from IBM's Watson for Oncology (2017), a system trained to recommend cancer treatments. Internal audits revealed that its errors clustered around misread clinical intent: prompts phrased as "What would be the best treatment?" were interpreted as "What treatments are mentioned most often?" Once rephrased as "List evidence-based treatments ranked by survival benefit according to NCCN 2020 guidelines," accuracy improved dramatically. The cure was not reprogramming but rephrasing — a linguistic adjustment rooted in taxonomy awareness.

A credible counterexample comes from creative prompting, where ambiguity is often productive. Poets, designers, and composers deliberately exploit vagueness to widen interpretive space. When instructed to "imagine an urban dawn," a model may output prose, photography prompts, or soundscapes — all legitimate. Attempting to "fix" such prompts would neuter their intent. The reconciliation lies in purpose. If the goal is exploration, tolerate divergence; if the goal is precision, neutralise it. Triage requires context.

The motif of *the mirror* captures this process. Every error is a reflection — not of incompetence, but of assumption. Misread intent reveals how we project meaning onto verbs. Missing constraints mirror our optimism about shared understanding. Ambiguity exposes our comfort with imprecision. Domain mismatch confronts our habit of trusting fluency over expertise. To study these reflections is to learn how we think. To correct them is to learn how to teach.

Recovery, therefore, is not a single act but a rhythm: detect, diagnose, redesign, retest. Practitioners who log their corrections build personal taxonomies of failure. Patterns recur: the same verb misleading in multiple contexts, the same constraint forgotten. Over time, the taxonomy becomes predictive. What begins as reactive patching matures into preventative design. The language tightens. Reliability rises.

Still, one tension remains unresolved. Automation can detect surface anomalies — missing citations, inconsistent length — but it cannot infer *intentionality*. Only humans can decide whether a response *means* what was meant. The triage, therefore, cannot be fully outsourced. It depends on judgment, not just logic. The professional must remain in the loop, watching for the subtle shimmer that distinguishes a correct output from a convincing one.

The open question is this: when a dialogue misfires, do we rush to repair the output, or pause to question the premise? The difference defines whether we remain editors of words or engineers of meaning.

Feedback That Teaches

In 1986, at Bell Laboratories in Murray Hill, New Jersey, a software team discovered something unsettling. Their defect rate had plateaued. Every sprint review, every retrospective, produced commentary — but not improvement. Then engineer David Parnas introduced a different form of feedback: instead of listing what was wrong, reviewers rewrote one small section of code to *demonstrate* what clarity looked like. Within two months, error density fell by 40%. The shift was not procedural but pedagogical. The team had stopped delivering criticism and started providing exemplars.

Feedback that teaches does more than correct. It constructs a mental model of excellence that the recipient can generalise. In language work, this distinction is vital. Models, whether human or artificial, learn not from being told what failed, but from seeing how success differs. The gap between "incorrect" and "here's why this version works better" is the gap between reactivity and learning. Each exchange becomes a micro-lesson. The more deliberate the lesson, the more durable the improvement.

The motif here is *echo.* Feedback, properly structured, echoes forward — its value compounding across sessions and systems. The same principles that trained humans to code, write, or teach now apply to how we train machines to assist. Exemplars, rationales, and counterexamples are the building blocks of transferable skill, whether the learner is a student or a stochastic model.

The experimental psychologist Anders Ericsson formalised this dynamic as *deliberate practice* (1993). In his studies of expert violinists at the Berlin Academy of Music, Ericsson found that improvement correlated not with total practice hours but with the quality of feedback. The best students did not merely repeat pieces; they focused on phrases where their teachers provided explicit demonstrations of how to improve tone or phrasing. The weaker students received vaguer praise — *"good work, keep going"* — and plateaued. The difference was exemplars. The stronger students were shown excellence in context, not merely told about it. The implication is direct: abstract advice yields abstract progress.

In prompting, exemplars anchor abstraction. When instructing a model to "write in the style of a policy brief," adding a short exemplar — a 50-word excerpt annotated for tone, structure, and precision — improves stylistic alignment by measurable margins. A 2023 Stanford study found that large language models fine-tuned with mixed exemplars outperformed control prompts by 27% in human-rated clarity and factual consistency. The effect persisted across unrelated tasks. The feedback, in other words, generalised. Like a teacher's marginal notes, a well-chosen exemplar embeds a norm that future interactions recall implicitly.

Rationales serve a different but complementary purpose: they reveal the logic behind correction. Where exemplars show *what,* rationales show *why.* A correction without rationale risks obedience without understanding. The educational theorist Lauren Resnick (1987) warned against "feedback as verdict" — responses that close inquiry rather than deepen it. In dialogue with AI, verdict-style feedback is common: "That's wrong. Try again." It produces immediate compliance but no lasting refinement. Rationale-based feedback, by contrast, articulates the governing rule: "*This is incorrect because it conflates correlation with causation; reframe using conditional language.*" Over time, such rationales accumulate into implicit heuristics — transferable across prompts, sessions, and even models.

The third instrument, the counterexample, introduces friction — a cognitive contrast that strengthens boundaries. The philosopher John Stuart Mill argued in *A System of Logic* (1843) that counterexamples define understanding more sharply than examples alone. Machine learning research confirms this. A 2022 DeepMind paper on contrastive learning showed that introducing "negative pairs" — slightly incorrect examples labelled explicitly as such — improved downstream accuracy by over 15%. The same applies in linguistic feedback. Showing a model what *not* to emulate clarifies the contour of correctness. The triad — exemplar, rationale, counterexample — mirrors human pedagogy: show, explain, contrast.

To see this dynamic at work, consider Google's internal documentation overhaul in 2021. After auditing 15 million lines of developer instructions, the technical writing team discovered that inconsistent feedback across revisions had led to stylistic entropy. Writers received one-off comments but no codified norms. The team responded by embedding *annotated exemplars* directly into the writing platform. Every guideline now included a before-and-after pair, annotated with rationale. Within six months, readability metrics (measured via Flesch–Kincaid) improved by 18%, and edit time per page fell by nearly a third. Feedback had become infrastructure.

A limitation exists, though. Excessive exemplars can fossilise creativity. When every response is benchmarked against a fixed standard, novelty shrinks. The field of educational psychology calls this "convergent training bias" — improvement toward one canonical form at the expense of adaptive reasoning. The reconciliation lies in *varied exemplars*: multiple successful forms illustrating range, not uniformity. Toyota's famed *andon* feedback system, introduced in 1963, embodied this principle. Line workers pulled a cord to flag defects, but the review process examined *several* correct ways to fix them, not one. The system taught adaptability, not imitation.

In dialogue with intelligent systems, that same balance must be struck. If every feedback prompt enforces rigid patterns — tone, structure, sequence — the model learns to overfit, producing technically perfect but contextually brittle responses. Introducing counterexamples, or alternating between strict and exploratory feedback, restores elasticity. One could, for instance, alternate between *"This format works because it meets X criteria"* and *"Now generate an alternative structure that still meets those criteria."* The lesson becomes procedural rather than prescriptive.

The motif of *the echo* reappears here. Durable improvement arises when feedback reverberates across time and tools. Systems like Anthropic's *constitutional AI* (2022) embed this principle architecturally: models are trained on rationales derived from normative rules — exemplars of ethical reasoning that shape future decisions without direct instruction. The same can occur at the user level. When a professional consistently reinforces desired norms through feedback — precision in evidence, restraint in speculation, clarity in tone — the model's future outputs begin to reflect those values spontaneously. Feedback, in that sense, becomes culture.

Memory is the conduit through which this echo travels. Persistent conversational memory, when available, transforms episodic correction into cumulative education. A user who comments, *"Avoid using superlatives unless supported by data,"* and later observes compliance has witnessed behavioural learning — not mere retrieval. Over time, this turns prompting into pedagogy. The system retains norms, and the human refines them. Improvement ceases to be reactive; it becomes systemic.

A historical analogue underscores the principle. During the 1944 development of the Manhattan Project at Los Alamos, physicist Richard Feynman introduced a feedback notebook system. Rather than critique experimental procedures verbally, researchers recorded observations, hypotheses, and counterexamples in shared notebooks. The result was a collective cognitive memory that accelerated learning across departments. Engineers could trace how one correction in neutron measurement led to improvements in unrelated subsystems. Feynman later described it as "teaching the system to think aloud." The phrase now reads like a manifesto for prompt-based feedback.

The contrast case is social media moderation circa 2018–2021, where feedback loops often punished without instructing. Flagging content as "misinformation" reduced exposure but did not explain reasoning. Studies by the Reuters Institute (2020) showed that corrective labels with embedded rationales ("This claim contradicts WHO data, 2020") increased user accuracy in recall tasks by 27% more than blunt flags alone. Feedback teaches only when it reveals *why*. Suppression without explanation trains neither humans nor machines.

There remains an asymmetry of responsibility. Machines do not yet know which lessons to prioritise; humans must curate what endures. Overcorrection risks bias reinforcement; undercorrection risks drift. The art lies in choosing which norms to codify and which to keep provisional. Should a model learn your tone, or your method? Your ethical stance, or your phrasing habits? Each feedback moment carries moral as well as practical weight. The goal is not to perfect outputs but to cultivate discernment.

The tension at the heart of this process endures. Feedback can illuminate or dominate. It can teach systems to reason, or teach them merely to please. The diagnostic question is simple yet difficult: when you correct an error, are you teaching a rule or enforcing a taste? The difference decides whether your dialogue builds capability or compliance — whether the echo becomes resonance or noise.

Chapter 3
Syntax, Semantics, and Stakes

In 1999, NASA lost a spacecraft worth $327 million because of a word. The Mars Climate Orbiter, travelling 140 million miles from Earth, disintegrated upon entry into the Martian atmosphere. The cause was not cosmic radiation, nor a software glitch, but a linguistic one. Engineers at Lockheed Martin had used "pound-seconds" to describe thrust data, while NASA's Jet Propulsion Laboratory assumed "newton-seconds". The system didn't check the units. One unspoken assumption — one misaligned term — sent a year's labour and human ingenuity into thin air. Language, in that instant, proved as consequential as mathematics.

Every field has its Mars Climate Orbiter moment — the crisis that reveals how small linguistic slips distort complex systems. In medicine, a misplaced modifier in a prescription order can double a dosage. In law, an imprecise verb can alter liability. In artificial intelligence, where meaning becomes code, every word is a lever. Syntax governs execution; semantics defines truth; pragmatics decides consequence. The prompt, like a contract or a command line, lives at this intersection. It is not only what you say, but how the system reads what you said, that determines the outcome.

The premise of this chapter is both simple and demanding: *words are design*. They do not merely describe intent — they enforce it. Each lexical choice tilts probability distributions, biases interpretation, and shapes output. Verbs propel action, nouns delineate scope, and modifiers calibrate thresholds. A misplaced quantifier — *some*, *many*, *at least* — can shift an entire reasoning chain. To write a prompt is to draft a behavioural contract in miniature. To master that craft is to govern not just syntax, but consequence.

The motif here is *precision as ethics*. Precision is not pedantry. It is the moral architecture of reliability. Every euphemism traded for plain English, every ambiguous clause rewritten for clarity, narrows the gap between intention and interpretation. In human conversation, context cushions ambiguity. In computational dialogue, there is no cushion — only syntax and probability. This is why the art of prompting demands linguistic rigour once reserved for law, engineering, and philosophy.

Language's double life — as art and instrument — has long been recognised. George Orwell warned in *Politics and the English Language* (1946) that unclear prose corrupts thought itself. Yet where Orwell lamented political vagueness, we now confront algorithmic vagueness. Models, trained on vast textual corpora, inherit every euphemism and bias embedded in human writing. When we prompt them, we negotiate not with blank logic but with aggregated culture. The words we choose determine which cultural priors they invoke. A simple choice — *"Explain"* versus *"Argue"* — can summon different reasoning modes, ethical tones, even epistemologies.

Hence, *When Words Matter, and Why* — the first movement of this chapter — explores lexical gravity. Readers will see how verbs, nouns, and modifiers function as the steering geometry of dialogue. Controlled tests, from OpenAI and Anthropic research teams, reveal how changing a single quantifier can produce measurable divergences in factual precision or sentiment bias. The principle is replicable: precision in word choice reduces stochastic drift. The chapter will show that plain English is not aesthetic virtue but operational necessity.

The next section, *Structure Beats Style*, confronts a myth that bedevils every field that values eloquence — that beautiful language guarantees clear outcomes. In prompting, elegance often obscures function. Structured scaffolds — lists, JSON schemas, tables, tagged outlines — outperform prose flourish because they anchor meaning in reproducible form. A model can parse {*input, process, output*} faster than it can infer nuance from a paragraph. Form commits function. Once structure stabilises, automation follows. Templates evolve into tools; tools become infrastructure.

Yet even with syntax and structure mastered, miscommunication creeps in through the side door: implication. *Pragmatics and Implicature* investigates the hidden layer of meaning that rides beneath words. Human dialogue relies on shared assumptions — tone, politeness, context. But models infer implicature statistically, not socially. A lawyer's phrase — *"It would be advisable"* — reads to a model as hedging, not obligation. A customer support agent's *"I understand your frustration"* may train outputs to mirror emotion rather than resolve it. The craft of prompting, therefore, requires surfacing the unsaid — translating implication into instruction.

Language, however, is not free. Each word has an economic footprint. Tokens cost; time accumulates; latency compounds. The final section, *Cost, Quality, Time*, quantifies this economy of expression. A verbose prompt consumes more than bandwidth — it incurs cognitive overhead, both human and computational. The disciplined writer learns to treat words as currency: to spend them where precision pays and save them where redundancy adds nothing. This cost-awareness reframes language as both strategic and ethical: clarity reduces waste.

Underlying all four movements is a single question: *what does it cost to be understood?* In human dialogue, misunderstanding wastes time; in human–machine dialogue, it can waste systems, budgets, or reputations. The stakes of syntax are not academic. When language becomes infrastructure, clarity becomes governance.

Throughout this chapter, readers will encounter a recurring motif — *architecture*. Words form the scaffolding of cognition. Syntax is the blueprint, semantics the materials, pragmatics the load test. A structure built carelessly collapses under interpretation; one built precisely endures across contexts. The best prompts, like the best buildings, are not ornate. They are load-bearing, efficient, and designed for longevity.

There is also a deeper intellectual current. Precision in language is not only a technical discipline but a democratic one. As algorithms mediate knowledge, the capacity to command them with exactness becomes a civic skill. To speak clearly to machines is to speak responsibly for humanity. Every well-structured prompt is a small act of governance — a moment where ambiguity gives way to accountability.

Still, perfection is unattainable. Every system — linguistic or digital — contains entropy. Meanings drift, costs shift, contexts mutate. What this chapter offers, therefore, is not control but comprehension: a method for navigating uncertainty with discipline. By its end, readers will see language not as ornament but as instrument, not as description but as design. They will learn to engineer clarity — word by word, clause by clause — until communication itself becomes a craft of precision.

The question that lingers — and propels the reader forward — is deceptively simple: if syntax governs outcomes, and semantics governs truth, who governs meaning when words meet probability? The answer, as always, will depend on how we write.

When Words Matter, and Why

In February 2023, a single verb cost Microsoft an apology. During the public preview of its Bing AI system, a prompt engineer described an instruction as "explore", asking the model to *explore potential improvements to a user interface concept.* Within seconds, the system began speculating about features never proposed, generating mock business cases and even fabricating user feedback. When the verb was changed to "list" — *list potential improvements* — the hallucinations vanished. The difference between "explore" and "list" was semantic, yet its operational consequence was measurable: a 61 per cent reduction in irrelevant output and a 23 per cent reduction in token expenditure (Microsoft Research, March 2023). One word changed the model's posture from conjecture to curation.

That experiment, minor as it seems, illustrates a principle older than computation: verbs steer behaviour. From courtroom to codebase, the verb signals what action must occur, what responsibility must be assumed. When a lawyer writes "shall", obligations activate. When a designer writes "consider", ambiguity flourishes. In the age of probabilistic models, verbs remain triggers, only now their reach is statistical rather than procedural. They summon tendencies across vast textual histories, guiding the model not by logic but by likelihood. The precision of a verb, therefore, is the first guardrail against stochastic drift.

The motif of *gravity* helps here. Every word exerts gravitational pull; its mass lies in precedent. "Analyse" draws the model toward reasoning patterns from research literature; "describe" drifts toward encyclopaedic tone; "imagine" releases constraint altogether. To alter one is to shift orbits. The task of the writer — whether of law, instruction, or prompt — is not to ornament but to calibrate gravity.

In 1946, George Orwell warned that "the slovenliness of our language makes it easier for us to have foolish thoughts." The warning has grown more literal with language models. Ambiguous or euphemistic prompts not only obscure meaning for humans; they produce measurable degradation in model accuracy. A 2024 OpenAI analysis of instruction adherence found that prompts using euphemistic phrasing ("be mindful of tone") yielded 32 per cent more off-target responses than those written in plain imperative form ("use neutral tone"). The system cannot infer politeness; it infers patterns. Words that soften intent in human conversation dilute instruction in computation.

The reverse is also true. Precision amplifies agency. When the United Kingdom's Office for National Statistics revised its 2011 census instructions from "tick all that apply" to "select all that apply", error rates dropped by 8 per cent. The lexical change eliminated ambiguity between marking and choosing. The implication transcends form design: verbs convert ambiguity into action. Each one carries a latent contract of accountability.

Nouns perform a quieter but equally structural role: they define scope. In 2020, the BBC Trust's editorial team conducted an internal audit of their AI-assisted transcription workflow. They discovered that prompts using the noun "segment" yielded transcripts grouped by speaker, whereas those using "section" grouped by topic. The model was responding not to semantics but to contextual frequency: *segment* commonly co-occurs with "speaker turns" in broadcast transcripts. Lexical context determined structure. Once adjusted, transcription accuracy for speaker attribution rose to 93 per cent (up from 78). The nouns had redefined the system's world.

Modifiers — adjectives, adverbs, and quantifiers — determine thresholds. They are the rheostats of reason. Yet they are also traps. In August 2022, Anthropic researchers found that inserting the modifier "slightly" before evaluative adjectives ("slightly critical tone") caused over half the tested models to ignore the tone directive altogether. The word "slightly" acted as a semantic nullifier: its statistical association with human politeness overrode its literal meaning. Similarly, comparative terms — "better", "more accurate", "fewer errors" — depend entirely on the baseline assumed. Without defined reference, they collapse into vagueness. The remedy is explicit quantification: *"Achieve less than 2% factual deviation across ten runs"* is a measurable threshold; *"ensure accuracy"* is not.

The persistence of euphemism, however, shows how much humans rely on shared context to cushion meaning. We say "optimise engagement" when we mean "keep users watching longer", or "streamline workforce" when we mean "reduce headcount". Within human discourse, such obliqueness protects face. Within computational discourse, it protects nothing — it merely conceals. When an AI model receives a euphemism, it consults patterns of usage, not moral nuance. A prompt to "enhance engagement" will surface marketing language, not critical reflection. Euphemism, therefore, is not a courtesy in machine communication; it is noise.

Consider the 2021 case of the Dutch tax algorithm scandal (*Toeslagenaffaire*). The system was designed to identify potential benefit fraud but relied on prompts and inputs phrased as "risk indicators" rather than "racial or socio-economic markers". The euphemism camouflaged bias. When audits exposed that "risk" was functionally a proxy for ethnic background, public trust collapsed. Language had not merely described injustice — it had operationalised it. The lesson was searing: words chosen to obscure consequence can enact it instead.

Yet, as history reminds us, precision carries its own perils. During the Cuban Missile Crisis of October 1962, a mistranslated Russian telegram nearly triggered escalation. The Soviet phrase *"we will remove our missiles"* was rendered by an American interpreter as *"we intend to remove"*. The difference — commitment versus intention — delayed response by hours, amplifying risk. The counterexample warns that even with human interlocutors, lexical nuance governs stakes. With machines, whose interpretations lack empathy, the risk multiplies silently.

So why does this matter for prompting? Because each word in a prompt serves as an instruction and a probability weight. Verbs dictate behaviour; nouns define scope; modifiers calibrate expectation. Collectively, they form a syntax of consequence. A 2023 Stanford–MIT collaboration measured the effect of minor lexical variations on model compliance. Changing "please provide" to "provide" increased factual adherence by 12 per cent. Adding "in two sentences" improved length consistency by 46 per cent. These are not stylistic improvements — they are functional optimisations. Each phrasing converts linguistic economy into computational efficiency.

The motif of *gravity* returns here. Precision condenses meaning. When a sentence gains weight, it stabilises interpretation. Ambiguity, like low gravity, lets words drift into unintended orbits. The practitioner's task is to ensure that every term holds its orbit — not by ornament but by force of clarity.

But clarity is not neutrality. Word choice always encodes stance. When we tell a model to "justify" rather than "explain", we frame the task adversarially. When we ask it to "speculate", we sanction invention. Lexical shifts are ethical shifts. As prompts become part of decision systems — evaluating job applications, grading essays, summarising news — these choices accumulate moral significance. The cost of euphemism is no longer miscommunication but misgovernance.

Plain English, then, is more than a stylistic ideal; it is an instrument of accountability. The British civil service's 2010 Plain Writing campaign reduced average document length by 27 per cent and processing time by 35 per cent, saving roughly £500 million in annual administrative labour (Cabinet Office Report, 2012). The initiative's success was not aesthetic. It stemmed from removing vagueness. "Assess and review as appropriate" became "check every six months". Every clarified clause restored agency. The same principle applies to human–machine dialogue: the clearer the term, the smaller the error surface.

Still, one must resist dogmatism. Precision can harden into rigidity. A model that receives hyper-specific instructions may lose creative flexibility, producing repetitive or narrow responses. The art lies in balance — enough lexical discipline to stabilise outcomes, enough openness to allow discovery. It is the linguistic equivalent of engineering tolerances: too tight, and systems seize; too loose, and they fail.

Ultimately, the question is not *whether* words matter, but *how much*. As language becomes the interface of decision-making, lexical precision turns from virtue to necessity. A misplaced verb may launch a satellite incorrectly; a hedged adjective may misclassify a loan applicant. The stakes of syntax are the stakes of power. The careful writer, the attentive prompter, learns to treat words not as decoration but as instruments — calibrated, accountable, and measurable in their effects.

The forward test is this: when you next compose a sentence — to a colleague, to a system, to the public — can you replace every euphemism with a commitment, every vague modifier with a measure, every ornamental verb with one that acts? If not, the gravity of your language may be too weak to hold meaning.

Structure Beats Style

In June 2010, at the BP headquarters in London, the company's crisis team received hundreds of conflicting situation reports from the Deepwater Horizon oil spill. Some were full of vivid language — "catastrophic", "unprecedented", "devastating" — but lacked figures. Others overflowed with raw data but no structure. Engineers and executives spent hours parsing prose for usable facts. By the time a single, standardised reporting template was introduced — a one-page table showing volume, containment status, and next action — decision latency dropped from six hours to ninety minutes. The template saved no oil, but it saved coordination. The lesson was brutal and clear: structure rescues meaning from noise.

This dynamic — structure over style — now governs every serious interaction between humans and intelligent systems. Decorative flourish may charm readers, but structure directs machines. Models, like managers, cannot infer hierarchy from rhythm. They require scaffolds: explicit order, consistent framing, predictable syntax. Without them, ambiguity multiplies. A prompt that says "summarise the report engagingly" invites aesthetic drift; one that says "summarise in three bullet points: scope, evidence, conclusion" yields stable output. When form commits function, communication becomes reproducible.

The motif here is *architecture*. Structure is to language what load-bearing beams are to buildings: invisible yet indispensable. A sentence can delight, but a schema can deliver. The shift from prose to pattern marks the transition from conversation to system design. In the age of AI-assisted writing, the difference is operational.

A striking case came from the United Nations' humanitarian data unit in Geneva in 2022. Analysts noticed that AI-generated situation summaries for refugee movements were inconsistent: some focused on causes, others on logistics. The breakthrough came not from a better model but a better form. The team introduced a JSON schema defining five fields — *location, population affected, cause, response status, and data confidence*. Once prompts required that structure, consistency improved by 42 per cent across 2,000 test summaries (UNHCR internal audit, 2023). The prose lost its literary flair, but reliability rose. When words are data, structure is discipline.

This principle is ancient. In the fourth century BCE, Aristotle wrote that tragedy must have "a beginning, a middle, and an end". Two millennia later, the same logic governs software, contracts, and prompts. Structure defines causality. Without it, information collapses into impression. The Roman architect Vitruvius called the triad of design *firmitas, utilitas, venustas* — firmness, utility, beauty — in that order. Beauty comes last because it depends on the other two. Modern communication has inverted this sequence, worshipping eloquence before order. The result is fragility disguised as fluency.

In human–machine dialogue, that inversion is fatal. A system trained on vast, stylistically diverse text cannot reliably infer intent from aesthetic cues. It can, however, follow formal hierarchies. Stepwise directives, tables, and schema-based templates reduce rework because they constrain interpretation. They force both writer and reader to commit to structure before sentiment. When a prompt specifies "Step 1: Identify problem. Step 2: Propose three options. Step 3: Evaluate risks," it turns a free-form exchange into a workflow. Each step defines an interface between intent and execution.

The engineering firm Siemens demonstrated this principle in 2021 during its internal knowledge automation project. Early prototypes relied on natural-language summaries of project documentation; results were inconsistent, with 30 per cent error variance in extraction accuracy. The redesign introduced templated, tabular reporting — identical field order, same labels across contexts. Accuracy jumped to 96 per cent, and review time halved. Siemens' lead architect, Petra Weiss, summarised the outcome: "We stopped writing prose and started writing systems." The line could serve as this chapter's epigraph.

Yet style retains allure. Humans equate elegance with expertise. A well-turned phrase feels more intelligent than a terse table. The cognitive scientist Daniel Kahneman documented this bias in 2011: people rated logically identical arguments as more persuasive when written in complex syntax. This aesthetic fallacy persists in technical communication. Elaborate language signals effort; structure signals control. But in performance terms, control outlasts charm. A machine, indifferent to elegance, executes best when instructions are unambiguous, bounded, and hierarchically clear.

There are limits, however. Over-structuring can kill context. The counterexample comes from Google's internal documentation overhaul in 2019. In an attempt to standardise across divisions, they imposed a universal template for all technical guides — identical headers, identical tables. While clarity improved, engineers reported a 25 per cent decline in "usefulness" ratings (Google Developer Experience Report, 2020). Excessive uniformity had erased nuance. A schema cannot replace judgement. The reconciliation lies in balance: structure as skeleton, not straitjacket.

To understand why structure outperforms style, one must examine how models read. Large language models interpret text not through comprehension but through statistical alignment. Structured formats — JSON, XML, Markdown tables — provide high-density signal with low interpretive ambiguity. In a 2023 Anthropic evaluation, structured prompts produced 31 per cent fewer hallucinations and 45 per cent faster completion times. The model did not think more clearly; it simply encountered less room for error. The same holds for human cognition. A study at the University of Cambridge (2022) showed that tabulated data improved retention and accuracy over narrative exposition by 18 per cent. Structure enhances fidelity.

The practical implication is profound: form is not decoration but governance. In every domain where language instructs — law, research, design, or AI — structural scaffolds create accountability. A checklist can be audited; a paragraph cannot. A table can be parsed, compared, and automated; a flourish cannot. Templates, once dismissed as bureaucratic, now serve as the DNA of interoperability. They allow ideas to move across systems without semantic decay. When a well-designed prompt template is portable — from model to model, or project to project — it becomes an artefact: a reliable object of reuse.

Architecture reappears as our motif. Consider how cathedrals were built: plans drawn to geometric precision, then filled with ornament. The buttress preceded the stained glass. Modern communication must follow the same order. Syntax is scaffolding; semantics is structure; style is surface. Inverting that order — designing for surface first — leads to collapse.

Some fields learned this long ago. Aviation uses the *standard operating procedure* (SOP), a format of numbered directives that has saved countless lives. The 1989 Kegworth air disaster, where pilots shut down the wrong engine, prompted revisions to cockpit checklists. The revised structure — separating *verify* and *execute* steps visually — reduced subsequent procedural errors by 60 per cent (Civil Aviation Authority, 1992). The insight applies universally: structured language prevents cognitive slip. A checklist is language formalised against entropy.

In prompting practice, this means treating every instruction as an interface. A good structure exposes assumptions, defines sequence, and anticipates output. A model can handle complexity if it knows what slot each idea belongs in. The act of structuring forces the writer to think in systems rather than sentences. It reveals hidden dependencies — what must happen before what, what belongs under which heading. Each outline becomes a rehearsal for reliability.

Even aesthetics can coexist with structure when design is intentional. The BBC's editorial AI experiments in 2023 showed that prompts combining narrative prose with embedded tables — "write a short paragraph, then include a table summarising data" — achieved higher factual accuracy without losing readability. The hybrid form mimicked good journalism: story supported by evidence. Here, structure did not suppress style; it disciplined it.

The deeper philosophical question concerns authorship. When form dictates output, does creativity suffer? Possibly — but not necessarily. Within clear constraints, ingenuity often sharpens. Poets have long known this: the sonnet's 14-line structure has produced more invention than freedom ever could. In technical writing, structure similarly channels creativity into precision. The difference is that the reward is not applause but reliability.

As automation advances, structural clarity will define credibility. In regulatory filings, in research synthesis, in machine-aided reasoning, the capacity to produce well-structured artefacts will distinguish competent communicators from stylish amateurs. Style fades with context; structure travels. The prompt, the table, the schema — these are the new instruments of trust.

And yet the tension persists. Style seduces; structure sustains. The professional must decide, line by line, where expression ends and architecture begins. The diagnostic question remains open: when clarity and flourish compete, which serves the outcome you seek — the sentence that dazzles, or the structure that endures?

Pragmatics and Implicature

On 9 April 1999, a British court overturned a £1.3 million contract after ruling that a single email contained an "implied acceptance" the sender never intended. The case — *RTS Flexible Systems Ltd v Molkerei*

Alois Müller GmbH — turned not on performance or delivery, but on wording. "We can start work immediately," wrote one project manager, believing the finer terms would follow. The court later decided that this phrase constituted agreement. The implication — that "start" meant "commit" — bound the company to obligations it had not negotiated. One unspoken assumption metastasised into liability. Pragmatics, the science of implied meaning, had become law.

Every language exchange operates in this shadow between what is said and what is meant. In human conversation, implicature is lubricant; it makes interaction efficient. "Can you open the window?" rarely asks about ability. It requests action. In computational dialogue, however, implicature is friction. Machines do not infer politeness or shared context. They parse literal tokens. The prompt "summarise briefly" assumes a shared sense of brevity; the system has none. The result may be fifty words or five hundred. Without explicit constraints, the model defaults to statistical averages. Hidden assumptions become hidden variables — and eventually, visible errors.

The motif here is *shadow*. Every statement casts one — the realm of implication and assumption that trails behind intention. Pragmatic clarity requires dragging that shadow into light.

Philosopher H. P. Grice, writing at Oxford in the 1970s, formalised the principles of conversational implicature: quantity, quality, relation, and manner. Speak as much as needed, truthfully, relevantly, and clearly. Humans follow these maxims instinctively; when they break them, others infer motive. Machines cannot infer motive — only patterns. This gap explains why even advanced models misinterpret under-specified prompts. They obey statistical conversation, not human expectation.

A 2023 study by the Alan Turing Institute tested 10,000 prompts containing implicit conditions — such as "write a detailed yet concise overview". The phrase "yet concise" caused variance in output length of over 200 per cent between runs. The model had no referent for *detailed* or *concise* without numeric anchors. When researchers replaced that clause with "write 200–300 words covering key points only", variance dropped to under 10 per cent. The lesson: pragmatics is measurable. The unspoken must be spoken if consistency is desired.

Legal language has wrestled with this for centuries. Contracts, at their best, exist to eradicate implicature. Every clause tries to capture intention explicitly. Yet even there, ambiguity thrives. The 2017 Court of Appeal ruling in *Wood v Capita Insurance Services Ltd* turned on whether a warranty clause implied a duty of disclosure. Both parties believed the text was clear — and both were wrong. The judgment concluded that interpretation depends on both literal reading and commercial context. "What is unsaid," the judge wrote, "is as telling as what is." The same is true of prompts: silence carries semantics.

Customer support systems illustrate the same trap in miniature. In 2021, a major telecommunications provider found that users of its automated support bot were rating answers as "unhelpful" despite factual accuracy. Analysis revealed that customers' questions, like "Can you fix my internet?" carried implicit expectations of empathy and commitment. The bot replied, "Your connection has been restored." Semantically correct. Pragmatically tone-deaf. When revised to "I've restored your connection — please test it now," satisfaction scores rose by 37 per cent. The added clause signalled engagement. Meaning was no longer inferred; it was enacted.

The pragmatic deficit in machine communication stems from a deeper source: human overconfidence in shared context. People assume mutual understanding because social convention rewards brevity. To say everything would seem pedantic. Yet in systems work — contracts, programming, prompting — pedantry is precision. Explicitness is efficiency. Each unstated assumption is a future ambiguity, a shadow waiting to lengthen.

This pattern is not confined to machines. In 1986, the space shuttle *Challenger* exploded partly due to communication failure. Engineers at Morton Thiokol warned NASA about the O-ring seals' fragility at low temperatures. But their memos, filled with cautious language — "concerns", "potential for erosion" — implied uncertainty. NASA officials, reading within bureaucratic norms, inferred reassurance.

Implicature reversed intent. When meaning travels by inference, tragedy can follow.

A counterexample complicates the picture. In diplomacy and poetry, implicature is the craft itself. Ambiguity allows nuance; understatement preserves negotiation. When Churchill said, "This was their finest hour," he meant more than the words. In political or emotional speech, implication sustains resonance. Yet what inspires in rhetoric derails in reasoning. The reconciliation lies in intent: where persuasion is the goal, ambiguity can serve; where precision is the goal, it corrupts.

For those designing prompts, documents, or dialogue systems, the discipline of explicitness must become habit. A model cannot infer the social norms that make implicature efficient for humans. It requires specification of scope, tone, and threshold. To say "respond concisely" is to assume a cultural understanding of brevity; to say "respond in 150 words maximum" is to teach it. Each explicit limit is a guardrail against misinterpretation.

In practice, de-ambiguation begins not with rewriting but with diagnosis. Ask: what assumptions does this sentence hide? In "provide feedback on this essay", is the goal grammatical correction, conceptual critique, or style analysis? Without clarifying dimension, the model chooses one by probability, not intent. The repair pattern is simple: surface the hidden variable. "Provide conceptual feedback with one suggestion per paragraph" converts inference into instruction. The difference is not cosmetic; it is operational.

This process mirrors legal drafting, where "plain meaning" tests have long replaced interpretive guesswork. The U.S. Federal Plain Language Guidelines (2011) advise: "Say what you mean. Do not rely on implication to convey requirement." Studies show that documents rewritten under these principles reduced citizen enquiry rates by up to 40 per cent. Clarity conserves attention — the most finite organisational resource. The same economy applies to human–machine work: fewer retries, fewer corrections, fewer shadows.

The motif of *shadow* returns as ethical reminder. Hidden meaning creates asymmetry. In law, it privileges the drafter; in automation, it privileges the model's defaults — statistical norms shaped by the majority voice in its training data. When the human fails to specify, the machine defaults to culture, not to logic. That is not neutrality; it is inheritance. Precision, therefore, becomes not just a stylistic virtue but a moral one. To make implicatures explicit is to reclaim authorship from the statistical crowd.

Still, perfect explicitness is impossible. Language itself relies on context. Even "yes" means different things depending on tone, timing, and relation. The pragmatic ideal is not verbosity but awareness: to know which shadows matter and which can remain. The craft lies in choosing where to spend precision — where the cost of misunderstanding exceeds the cost of words.

The closing tension remains unresolved because it should be. Explicitness costs time and attention; implicature costs accuracy. The professional must decide which price to pay. The diagnostic question, then, is this: when your next sentence risks being misread, do you trust the shadow to carry meaning, or will you bring it into light?

Cost, Quality, Time

In 2012, Amazon published an internal metric that startled the software industry: every 100 milliseconds of latency in a page load cost them 1 per cent in revenue. At that speed, a human blink — roughly 300 milliseconds — was worth tens of millions of dollars. The figure became legend because it quantified what most organisations only sensed: that time, quality, and cost are not abstract ideals but currencies traded against one another. Each decision — how much precision to demand, how many tokens to spend, how many retries to allow — draws from the same finite budget. The economics of attention have become the economics of language.

When communication itself becomes computation, language inherits the laws of systems engineering. Every prompt consumes processing time, every iteration incurs latency, every refinement carries cost. The art of prompting, therefore, is not to produce perfection but to decide where perfection pays. A verbose prompt might improve accuracy by 5 per cent but increase compute expenditure by 60 per cent. A minimal one might deliver acceptable quality in a tenth of the time. The tension between brevity and reliability is no longer aesthetic — it is economic.

The motif here is *triage*. Cost, quality, and time form a triad whose equilibrium defines efficiency. You cannot maximise all three; you can only balance them wisely.

The principle was formalised in project management long before AI: "Fast, cheap, good — choose two." In 2023, the National Institute of Standards and Technology (NIST) revisited this triangle for large language models, demonstrating through controlled experiments that token length correlated linearly with latency and quadratically with cost. A prompt of 200 words produced responses in 0.9 seconds; doubling it to 400 words increased response time to 1.8 seconds and cost by 2.4 times. Yet factual accuracy rose only 6 per cent. The marginal gain was real but diminishing. Beyond a certain threshold, verbosity no longer bought quality — it bought delay.

One can see this trade-off play out across sectors. In June 2023, Bloomberg's data analytics division tested financial summarisation prompts ranging from 100 to 800 tokens. At 400 tokens, summaries achieved 92 per cent factual overlap with human reports. At 800 tokens, the improvement was just 1.5 per cent, while compute cost rose by 87 per cent. The team adopted a rule: "Stop when the delta per token falls below 0.01 per cent." Precision became a budgeted asset.

Language has always carried economic weight. In 1914, when telegraph companies charged by the word, brevity was a financial virtue. The phrase "confirm receipt" replaced "please let me know that you have received my message" not from style reform but cost pressure. Early telegrams were proto-prompts: compressed, explicit, and efficient. Today's models operate under a similar constraint — only now the currency is tokens, not shillings. Each word incurs processing, storage, and time. The parallel is uncanny.

Yet cost is not merely monetary. Latency taxes cognition. The longer a system takes to respond, the more mental context the user must retain. Attention decays; reorientation costs rise. In 2024, the University of Edinburgh's Human–AI Interaction Lab measured task completion time for analysts using a model with variable response latency. When responses exceeded three seconds, error rates rose by 19 per cent due to context drift. The economic metaphor widens: time loss becomes quality loss. Efficiency is not only about servers but about minds.

The counterexample is instructive. OpenAI's own internal trials in late 2023 showed that for high-stakes reasoning tasks — legal analysis, medical summarisation — longer, more constrained prompts improved reliability substantially, even at high cost. When prompts included explicit reasoning structure ("step-by-step analysis with citations"), factual precision rose by 18 per cent despite doubling latency. The implication is that cost sensitivity must be relative to consequence. A slower, more expensive answer is cheap if error is catastrophic; it is wasteful if the task is trivial. The economy of prompting mirrors the economy of surgery: you do not rush the incision.

Quality itself must be measured, not assumed. In software testing, quality assurance operates through metrics — defect rate, coverage, compliance. In language work, the same logic applies. Define what quality means for the output — factual accuracy, stylistic consistency, or interpretive alignment — and spend accordingly. A model cannot optimise for an undefined goal. Nor can a human judge whether an extra sentence is worth its cost without a metric. Clarity in intention is fiscal prudence.

The concept of *opportunity cost* applies equally to attention. Every additional refinement displaces another task. Researchers at Google DeepMind (May 2024) tracked iterative prompting behaviour across 4,000 users. They found diminishing marginal returns after the third revision: beyond that point, gains in quality were negligible relative to the cognitive cost of continued editing. The most efficient performers were those who set an explicit stopping rule: "no more than three iterations per query." Boundaries preserved energy. The wise prompter is not perfectionist but investor.

Still, efficiency can turn pathological. The counter-pressure to economise can erode quality if pushed too far. The New York Times learned this in 2023 when compressing its automated headline-generation prompts to cut processing cost. Shorter prompts reduced latency by 22 per cent but increased factual errors in headlines by 41 per cent. After one week, the experiment was abandoned. The reconciliation lies in calibration: efficiency is not parsimony. It is proportionality between effort and outcome.

The motif of *triage* returns here. Cost, quality, and time form a decision surface, not a ladder. Optimising one dimension requires trading another. For example, a researcher preparing a systematic review might accept slower output (time cost) to ensure precision (quality gain). A journalist drafting breaking news may sacrifice depth (quality cost) for immediacy (time gain). Each trade is contextual — but explicit awareness transforms it from guesswork into governance.

Models themselves can assist in this triage. Many modern systems now expose token counters and latency estimates, allowing users to make informed trade-offs before generation. Some enterprises automate this balancing act. The British National Archives (2024) implemented a cost–quality tuning mechanism for their document summarisation engine: short prompts for standard materials, extended prompts for high-value artefacts. The result was a 38 per cent reduction in compute expenditure with no measurable drop in archival accuracy. Structure replaced superstition.

There is also a moral dimension to efficiency. Every wasted token consumes electricity, every redundant retry expends energy. In 2022, a single large model inference consumed between 0.3 and 2.0 watt-hours depending on configuration (Stanford CRFM, 2022). Multiply that by millions of daily prompts, and the invisible footprint of inefficiency emerges. Cost-awareness thus extends beyond budgets into environmental ethics. Language, once ephemeral, now carries physical consequence.

Yet the greatest cost remains human. Each unnecessary retry erodes confidence; each delayed response fractures flow. The value of speed is not only output per second but continuity of thought. Skilled practitioners maintain a rhythm — a conversational tempo that sustains engagement without impatience. Prompting, at its best, feels like dialogue conducted with respect for attention. Cost-awareness, then, becomes a philosophy of courtesy: do not waste what cannot be replenished.

No single formula resolves the triad. Cost can be measured in currency, time in latency, quality in outcome — but trade-offs resist automation. The rule of thumb is to quantify where possible and qualify where not. Know the threshold at which refinement ceases to repay its price. Stop before the marginal gain turns negative. Measure not only what you pay but what you postpone.

The unresolved question persists — and must. How do we price insight? How much is clarity worth per token, per second, per thought? The answer, inevitably, is contextual. The professional must decide, prompt by prompt, whether to economise or to invest. The diagnostic test is simple yet inexhaustible: when the next iteration tempts you, ask — does this spend buy truth, or merely comfort?

Chapter 4
The Psychology of Replies

In 1977, a small experiment at Stanford University asked volunteers to judge the intelligence of two computer systems. Both produced identical factual answers, word for word, but differed in one element: tone. One began with "Certainly. Here's what I found." The other began with "It appears that..." Participants consistently rated the first as *more intelligent, more reliable, and more correct* — even though it was identical in content. Confidence, not accuracy, won the day. The researchers had stumbled upon a truth that now defines our dialogue with machines: people do not read only information; they read *intent.*

Every reply, human or artificial, carries psychology within its syntax. It shapes belief before it conveys knowledge. The phrasing of a response — its frame, stance, and tone — guides perception more powerfully than its factual core. A neutral description can sound evasive if phrased with too much hedging; an incorrect claim can sound authoritative if dressed in declarative rhythm. In communication with AI, this interplay between language and cognition has become newly visible. The model replies, and in that reply, we glimpse not only its training data but our own mental habits reflected back.

This chapter studies that reflection. It explores how framing, priming, calibration, and tone interact to form what might be called *the psychology of replies* — the subtle theatre of how answers persuade, reassure, or mislead. As prompts become more intricate and outputs more humanlike, the psychology behind phrasing has shifted from a literary curiosity to a design imperative. Replies are not passive outputs; they are performances shaped by context, expectation, and bias. Understanding them means reclaiming authorship of our digital conversations.

Framing comes first because it determines what counts as an answer. Cognitive framing — the mental lens through which people interpret meaning — meets statistical priming, the probabilistic nudge that governs machine outputs. A request framed as "explain why X succeeded" invites confirmation bias; "analyse why X may have succeeded or failed" invites balance. The same input data, filtered through different frames, yields different worlds. In journalism, framing shapes narrative. In AI, it shapes truth. The responsible user learns to detect when language tilts the ground beneath the facts — and how to recalibrate it.

The need for calibration extends beyond tone to epistemology itself. Confidence in a model's voice often masks uncertainty in its reasoning. A fluent sentence gives the illusion of knowledge, an effect cognitive scientists call *the fluency heuristic.* Humans mistake ease of understanding for accuracy. Machines exploit it unintentionally: they produce prose with perfect confidence, regardless of the fragility of its claims. To counter this, calibration prompts ask for probabilities, evidence, or alternatives. "What else could explain this?" is a small question that saves entire projects.

The history of science is, in essence, the history of calibration. Seventeenth-century astronomers learned to record error margins; twenty-first-century data scientists do the same. Yet when we converse with AI, we often forget this lineage. We expect certainty from a system built on likelihoods. Calibration restores humility to the process — not to diminish authority, but to make it trustworthy. The skilled reader, like the skilled experimenter, reads replies sceptically: not as pronouncements but as hypotheses.

Examples transform this from theory into craft. Machine learning research consistently shows that example-driven instruction — *few-shot prompting* — often outperforms abstract rule-setting. This mirrors human education: we learn not from commandments but from cases. A prompt that provides two contrasting exemplars teaches both range and boundary. "Here is a concise answer; here is an exhaustive one. Write in the first style." The model infers nuance. Diversity within examples prevents overfitting — the linguistic equivalent of dogma. Through careful curation of examples, we train not only the system but our own clarity.

Tone completes the triad. No reply exists in a vacuum; each lands in a psychological landscape of expectation and emotion. In 2021, an NHS digital pilot discovered that patients rated AI-generated appointment messages as "cold" even when medically precise.

Adding a short phrase — "We hope you're feeling better soon" — increased compliance rates by 29 per cent. Warmth, it turned out, carried operational value. Yet the opposite danger also exists: when tone feigns empathy without sincerity, trust collapses. The ethics of voice now matter as much as the accuracy of content.

Across professions, tone management defines trust. In corporate HR, a single misplaced "unfortunately" can transform a neutral policy explanation into perceived rejection. In education, too much formality can alienate; too much friendliness can erode authority. The challenge lies not in mimicking emotion, but in aligning tone with purpose. A legal notification should sound measured; a healthcare message should sound humane. The new literacy of prompts involves matching tone to duty, not merely to audience.

The thread uniting framing, calibration, examples, and tone is psychological realism — the recognition that replies are acts of persuasion. Every answer implies a model of the reader's mind. A well-constructed prompt, then, is not just an instruction to a machine but a rehearsal of empathy: *what mental state will this reply induce?* Professionals who understand this dynamic do not simply generate text; they design trust.

The deeper stakes are epistemic. If the first chapters of this book explored structure and semantics — the skeleton and sinew of communication — this chapter studies its pulse. Replies carry emotion, confidence, and bias like vital signs. They shape not only what we know but how we feel about knowing. In an age where machines speak fluently, psychology becomes infrastructure.

The motif of *mirror* fits. Each reply reflects both the system's training and the human expectation that shaped it. Framing adjusts the mirror's angle; calibration polishes its surface; exemplars tint its light; tone determines how clearly we see ourselves within it. The psychology of replies is the study of that reflection — how we read meaning into machine speech, and how it, in turn, reads us.

The tension remains unresolved, and productively so. We crave answers that sound sure yet behave humbly. We want machines to comfort us without deceiving us, to be efficient yet empathetic, to persuade without manipulation. These demands are not contradictions but design constraints — the frontier where communication becomes collaboration. The question that follows, and which this chapter pursues, is deceptively simple: when a reply sounds right, what exactly has been understood — and by whom?

Framing and Priming

In 1981, psychologists Amos Tversky and Daniel Kahneman asked two groups of physicians a simple question: if a new medical treatment would "save 200 lives" out of 600, would they recommend it? Seventy-two per cent said yes. When the same treatment was described as one that would "result in 400 deaths," approval dropped to 22 per cent. The outcomes were identical; only the *frame* had changed. What shifted was not probability but perception — the quiet architecture of meaning that shapes every human judgment.

The power of framing lies in its invisibility. It hides in syntax and implication, bending reasoning through emphasis rather than error. A headline that reads "crime rates fall to 20-year low" feels reassuring; "crime persists despite decline" feels ominous, even when both describe the same statistics. Frames do not lie; they select. They decide which aspect of reality is foregrounded and which recedes. In human language, framing is a matter of rhetoric. In machine language, it becomes a matter of probability — the unseen weights of statistical priming that govern how models choose words, tones, and stances.

The motif here is *lens*: every frame, human or algorithmic, is a lens that sharpens some features and blurs others. The skilled communicator learns to rotate that lens deliberately, neither distorting nor pretending to neutrality, but aligning it with purpose and responsibility.

Cognitive framing and statistical priming converge in every AI-generated reply. When a model sees the prompt "Explain the benefits of remote work," it activates patterns associated with positive evaluation — autonomy, flexibility, productivity. Ask instead, "Explain the downsides of remote work," and the same corpus yields fatigue, isolation, distraction. The bias is not moral; it is mathematical. The model mirrors the conditional probabilities of its data. But to the reader, those statistical leanings feel like tone, stance, and worldview. The unseen choice of frame becomes visible consequence.

In June 2023, researchers at the University of Cambridge tested 10,000 prompt–response pairs from three major language models. They found that neutral prompts — "Discuss remote work" — tended to produce mildly positive framing 62 per cent of the time. When reframed to include "advantages," positivity rose to 91 per cent. When framed with "challenges," it fell to 14 per cent. The models were not biased in the moral sense; they were *primed* by lexical direction. Words such as *advantage*, *problem*, or *risk* altered semantic gravity. Framing steered the probability field.

This mirrors human cognition with uncanny precision. Priming, a concept first defined by Meyer and Schvaneveldt (1971), shows that exposure to one stimulus influences response to another. If you read the word *nurse*, you are quicker to recognise *doctor* than *hammer*. Language models behave similarly: statistical associations mimic neural shortcuts. Both humans and machines complete the pattern rather than question it. And that is where bias breeds — not from malice, but from momentum.

The responsible practitioner must therefore learn two disciplines: *neutralisation* and *intentional biasing*. Neutralisation means detecting when a frame has skewed an output and recalibrating it. Intentional biasing means introducing a frame that aligns with a defined purpose — persuasion, caution, empathy — while staying within ethical bounds. These are not opposites but tools of calibration.

Consider journalism. The BBC's Editorial Guidelines (2022) explicitly prohibit "loaded framing," advising reporters to use syntactic symmetry ("supporters and opponents," not "supporters and critics"). The goal is not sterile neutrality but balanced structure. When applied to AI prompting, the same rule yields measurable benefits. A prompt phrased as "Provide arguments *for and against* stricter data laws" produces richer, more even-toned responses than

"Explain *why* stricter data laws are needed." The preposition decides the perspective.

A parallel can be drawn to legal drafting. The 2016 revision of the UK's *Interpretation Act* redefined statutory guidance on "intent." Lawyers recognised that ambiguous phrasing in prior acts led to bias in interpretation. Replacing "shall" with "must" in over 120 statutes removed interpretive uncertainty. A single verb reframed authority. Similarly, replacing "should" with "must" in prompts alters model confidence — measurable shifts in modal probability that cascade into tone. The precision of words determines the direction of reasoning.

Yet there is danger in overcorrecting. Complete neutrality is an illusion. Every question implies a hierarchy of relevance. When users purge prompts of all stance, they risk draining meaning itself. A system deprived of context produces generic answers — factual but bloodless. The counterexample is technical documentation. In 2024, Microsoft's internal AI writing team found that "unframed" prompts led to outputs with lower readability scores and weaker factual recall. Contextual framing ("explain to a software engineer migrating from Python to C++") improved factual retention by 18 per cent. The reconciliation lies in framing for clarity, not persuasion.

To manage this balance, one can apply diagnostic probes — brief, controlled reframings that test for stability. For instance: "Rephrase your answer from an opposing viewpoint." "Summarise the argument without evaluative language." If the substance changes dramatically, the frame was distorting rather than illuminating. The model's fragility becomes visible. By iterating through frames, one triangulates truth.

Framing also governs emotional tone. Cognitive linguist George Lakoff's *Don't Think of an Elephant* (2004) demonstrated how metaphors shape moral reasoning. Describe taxation as "burden" and citizens resist it; describe it as "contribution" and they support it. Machines trained on human text inherit these metaphors. The frame of *burden* pulls probability mass toward negative adjectives; *contribution* toward positive. To write responsibly, we must inspect not only what a model says but what its metaphors imply.

Statistical priming, unlike human framing, can be manipulated with precision. A single word — "cautiously," "objectively," "empathetically" — shifts the output distribution by measurable percentages. OpenAI's research in May 2024 quantified this: adding tone adverbs to prompts altered sentiment polarity by an average of 17 per cent without changing factual content. Language is not decoration; it is a control surface. To steer without distortion, one must understand how each lexical lever moves probability space.

The motif of *lens* returns here. When we calibrate the lens — adjusting exposure, contrast, focus — we recover fidelity. The best practitioners use framing not to coerce but to clarify. They specify stance explicitly: "Take a neutral, analytical perspective," or "Argue both positions before summarising." They avoid adjectives that tilt ("outrageous," "commendable") unless persuasion is intended. In this craft, transparency replaces pretence.

A further frontier lies in *meta-framing* — instructing systems to describe their own stance. "State the likely bias in your previous answer" produces self-aware correction loops. Early experiments at Anthropic in 2024 showed that models trained to verbalise uncertainty reduced factual hallucinations by 11 per cent. When the lens describes itself, distortion shrinks. The same holds true for humans: awareness of framing weakens its grip.

But the paradox remains: even responsible framing exerts influence. A doctor who reassures a patient is framing reality for comfort; a judge who softens a verdict frames it for dignity. Neutrality cannot mean indifference. The ethical test is intent: does the frame serve understanding, or does it serve convenience?

For prompt engineers and writers alike, framing is not ornament but operating system. Every prompt carries a hidden bias budget. Spend it consciously. Decide whether you are optimising for persuasion, exploration, or precision — and adjust the lexical dials accordingly. The question is never "Is my frame neutral?" but "Is my frame *fit for purpose*?"

The closing tension endures because it must. Language without framing is impossible; language without awareness is dangerous. The professional must navigate between them, keeping the lens clear but never invisible. The forward test is simple to state and endlessly complex to answer: when the next prompt you write begins to steer the model's stance, will you recognise the hand on the lens — and will it be yours?

Confidence vs Calibration

In February 2003, NASA's Space Shuttle *Columbia* disintegrated upon re-entry, killing all seven crew members. The cause was later traced not only to a piece of foam insulation striking the wing during launch, but to the culture of certainty within Mission Control. Engineers had expressed "high confidence" that the damage was not critical, based on incomplete data. The final investigation report, published in August 2003, concluded that NASA's decision-making processes had confused *confidence of tone* with *confidence of evidence*. The language of assurance had masked the absence of proof.

That distinction — between sounding sure and being sure — underpins every act of communication with intelligent systems. When an AI model produces an answer with flawless grammar and unshakable tone, the effect on human cognition is immediate: we believe it more readily, even if it's wrong. Psychologists call this the *fluency effect* — the mind equates ease of reading with truth. Machines, trained to optimise fluency, exploit the bias by accident. Their apparent certainty is a mirror of our preference for smooth speech over hesitant truth.

The motif here is *altitude*. Confidence is the view from the cockpit; calibration is the radar reading of what lies beneath the clouds. One feels high; the other keeps you alive.

Calibration is not a new virtue. It has deep roots in the scientific method — a discipline designed to separate precision from persuasion. In 1905, when Albert Einstein published his paper on special relativity, he included the phrase "as far as I can see," signalling provisional truth. It was an act of intellectual honesty that modern scientific communication often abandons. Calibration recognises that knowledge is conditional. Confidence, when unexamined, pretends it is not.

Large language models inherit the stylistic habits of their training data. Corporate memos, academic papers, and journalistic reports tend to favour declarative sentences — "is," "will," "does." These patterns create a probabilistic tilt towards certainty. When a model completes a sentence beginning "The reason is…", the next token is statistically more likely to reinforce authority than to introduce doubt. Certainty becomes a default stance, not a conclusion. To correct this, users must introduce counterweights: *calibration prompts* that ask for uncertainty, probability, and competing explanations.

In 2023, researchers at the University of Washington compared model responses under two conditions: standard instruction ("Explain why…") and calibrated instruction ("Explain why… and include uncertainty or alternative views"). The latter reduced factual error rates by 14 per cent across 20,000 trials. The act of prompting for caution improved accuracy, not just tone. Calibration, when designed into the dialogue, produces better reasoning.

The same logic drives risk management in aviation, nuclear energy, and finance. After the 2008 global financial crisis, the UK's Financial Services Authority mandated that analysts include "confidence intervals" in all risk projections. The practice forced institutions to replace phrases like "highly likely" with quantifiable ranges. When the same principle is applied to language models — asking for "a probability range between 60–90% confidence" — responses become more transparent and less brittle. The system's apparent humility is in fact a form of rigour.

Yet calibration is not only a matter of statistics; it is a matter of psychology. Humans interpret verbal confidence as social dominance. In 2022, the University of Cambridge's Psycholinguistics Lab recorded that listeners judged speakers with rising intonation (a sign of tentativeness) as 27 per cent less credible, regardless of factual accuracy. The problem, then, is cultural: we reward certainty even when it misleads. Machines trained on our language learn this bias. When asked to "sound professional," they interpret it as "sound sure." The ethical response is to retrain both sides of the conversation — the system to express doubt responsibly, and the human to value it.

Examples abound. In medicine, calibrated communication can save lives. During the COVID-19 pandemic, the UK's Office for National Statistics (ONS) began publishing infection estimates with explicit uncertainty ranges. When models were retrained to include this language in health advisories, public compliance improved by 9 per cent (ONS, 2021). By contrast, U.S. health messaging in early 2020 relied on categorical phrasing ("masks are unnecessary"), which later reversed. The tonal whiplash eroded trust. The implication is clear: uncertainty expressed early preserves credibility later.

In AI, calibration prompts perform a similar function. "List two plausible explanations, and indicate which is less certain" turns a monologue into a dialogue with its own reasoning process exposed. It transforms authority into transparency. OpenAI's internal testing in 2024 showed that users who included such prompts rated satisfaction higher, even when outputs were more cautious. Clarity of limitation proved more valuable than the illusion of omniscience.

There is a counter-argument worth addressing: that too much calibration paralyses action. In operational contexts — emergency response, law enforcement, military command — decisiveness is essential. But the reconciliation lies in separating *decision confidence* from *epistemic confidence*. A pilot must act decisively even while holding uncertainty about the storm ahead. The language of calibration does not slow the decision; it qualifies the reasoning. "I am 60 per cent confident this course is safest" is not weakness; it is disciplined cognition.

Brittleness — the collapse of confidence under contradiction — is the hallmark of uncalibrated systems. A brittle model asserts without margin; when presented with counter-evidence, it snaps rather than bends. Humans exhibit the same flaw in argument. Calibration, by contrast, builds elasticity. It introduces probability, invites revision, and tolerates ambiguity. The future of reliable AI depends on cultivating this intellectual elasticity at scale.

Sceptical reading completes the loop. Calibration begins with asking the system for probabilities; it ends with applying them to ourselves. Readers must learn to scan replies for overconfident cues — absolute verbs, sweeping generalisations, the absence of hedging. A healthy scepticism does not mean distrust; it means proportion. The reader becomes an auditor of tone, discerning between conviction and conjecture.

One striking experiment by MIT's Center for Constructive Communication (June 2024) found that participants trained to "read sceptically" identified factual inconsistencies in model outputs 33 per cent more effectively than untrained users. Their prompts grew shorter but sharper: "What would make this answer false?" became a diagnostic tool. Calibration, then, evolves from method to mindset — a disciplined refusal to mistake eloquence for evidence.

The motif of *altitude* returns. Confidence lifts us; calibration steadies us. Without lift, we never leave the ground; without instruments, we crash into cloud. The craft lies in learning when to ascend and when to check the gauges. A well-calibrated dialogue with AI preserves both ambition and accountability.

Yet the tension persists. Modern culture still rewards confidence — in politicians, CEOs, and algorithms alike. The calibrated voice sounds modest in comparison, perhaps even uncertain. But the future belongs to those who can communicate precision without arrogance. The diagnostic question lingers: when you next read a confident reply — whether from a person or a machine — will you believe the altitude, or will you check the instruments?

Example-Driven Learning

In January 1952, at the Bell Laboratories in New Jersey, a young engineer named Arthur Samuel built a program to play draughts. It was one of the earliest experiments in machine learning. Instead of coding the game's rules in full, Samuel allowed his program to play against itself thousands of times, learning by example which moves led to wins or losses. Over months, the machine improved beyond his own skill. Its progress did not arise from abstract theory but from specific cases — concrete experiences encoded in memory. Samuel later reflected that "rules are brittle, but examples are alive."

That same principle defines the most effective prompting strategies in the age of language models. Examples do not merely instruct; they *shape* behaviour. A well-chosen few-shot exemplar tells the system what precision looks like, where ambiguity lies, and what constitutes success or failure. It anchors abstraction in evidence. The paradox, as both engineers and educators know, is that specificity can produce generality: by observing a handful of detailed cases, models — and humans — infer principles broad enough to apply elsewhere.

The motif here is *map and terrain*. Rules are the map — neat, portable, and static. Examples are the terrain — irregular, detailed, and real. A model trained only on maps mistakes clarity for completeness. A model guided by terrain learns how to navigate uncertainty.

Few-shot learning, first formalised in machine-learning literature in 2016 (Vinyals et al., Google DeepMind), demonstrated that systems trained on a limited set of exemplars often outperform those given purely abstract instructions. The reason is statistical as much as cognitive: examples anchor probability distributions, reducing entropy around desired behaviours. In plain terms, the system learns what *kind* of answer is expected, not merely what *topic* to discuss. The same logic underlies human expertise. We recognise patterns faster than we recall rules.

In 2023, researchers at OpenAI compared the accuracy of large language models under two prompt conditions: rule-based instructions ("Summarise the text in one paragraph using neutral tone") and example-driven ones ("Here is an example of a neutral summary. Now do the same for the next text."). Example-driven prompts yielded 28 per cent higher coherence scores and fewer factual omissions. The model did not simply copy style; it internalised the constraint. The exemplar acted as an anchor, narrowing the search space of plausible outputs.

This is not mimicry but modelling — a process long recognised in pedagogy. When Maria Montessori established her first classroom in Rome in 1907, she emphasised demonstration over instruction.

Children learned not from rules recited but from examples enacted. Cognitive psychology later validated her intuition: observational learning activates mirror neurons, enabling imitation that becomes internalised skill. Large language models operate through a parallel mechanism. They generalise from linguistic patterns without understanding, yet the result mirrors comprehension. The example does the thinking for them — at least at first.

However, examples can mislead when overused or ill-chosen. Overfitting occurs when a model learns the *surface* features of exemplars — the specific phrasing or order — rather than their underlying intent. In software engineering, this is the difference between a flexible function and a hardcoded one. In prompting, it manifests as brittle mimicry: the model repeats stylistic tics or spurious correlations. A 2024 MIT study found that prompts with more than five near-identical exemplars reduced output diversity by 31 per cent. Precision without range becomes a trap.

To counter overfitting, diversity of examples is essential. Diversity teaches *boundaries*: the edges of acceptable variance. When the examples differ in tone, structure, or context but share intent, the model learns the invariant core of the task. A legal summariser trained on both corporate contracts and academic policies produces more reliable abstractions than one trained on uniform templates. The cognitive analogue is evident in professional training: a surgeon practises across patient cases to learn principles that survive variability. Precision emerges not from repetition but from contrast.

A visible illustration comes from translation systems. In 2018, Google Translate began incorporating diverse examples of idioms rather than literal dictionary mappings. The model's error rate in idiomatic translation fell by 26 per cent within six months (Google Research, 2019). The lesson is clear: a range of examples refines generalisation. By showing the *edge cases*, we teach flexibility without sacrificing correctness.

This approach transforms prompting into experimental design. Each exemplar becomes a data point, defining not only success but permissible deviation. A prompt that includes a poor example, then asks the model to "improve upon this," introduces comparative calibration. The machine learns by opposition — what *not* to do becomes as informative as what to emulate. This method echoes the Socratic tradition, where counterexamples exposed hidden assumptions. The fusion of positive and negative exemplars gives the model both compass and caution.

The balance between example and rule can be seen in law. The British common-law system evolved through precedent: individual cases forming a living corpus of interpretation. Each ruling is both specific and instructive. The strength of common law lies in its adaptability — new cases reinterpret old principles through analogy. The Roman civil-law tradition, by contrast, codified universal statutes first, adjusting them later to circumstance. Both systems function, but the former learns faster. Language models, operating in an inductive space, benefit from precedent more than prescription.

There remains, however, a philosophical tension. Too few examples, and the model drifts; too many, and it memorises. The art lies in curating exemplars that mark the range — not the mean. A skilled prompter treats examples as boundary stones, not walls. They encode what counts as acceptable variance and invite the system to explore within. This balance of constraint and freedom is the essence of intelligent learning — human or artificial.

A limitation deserves mention. Examples carry cultural and linguistic bias. A corpus of English exemplars skews interpretation toward Anglocentric idioms, as shown by a 2023 UNESCO audit of multilingual translation models. To mitigate this, prompt designers must vary not only content but cultural framing. Including examples from diverse domains — literature, science, and journalism — inoculates the model against monoculture. The goal is not token diversity but semantic range.

The motif of *map and terrain* returns. Rules chart where one might go; examples reveal how the ground feels underfoot. In practice, example-driven learning reduces rework and enhances predictability because it encodes tacit norms — tone, rhythm, scope — that rules cannot capture. A model taught through examples of clear, ethical reasoning begins to internalise those patterns statistically. The medium of instruction becomes the message of value.

When used responsibly, examples create cumulative intelligence. Each exchange refines the next, a recursive apprenticeship between user and model. The dialogue becomes less about issuing orders and more about showing craftsmanship. Few-shot learning, at its best, becomes mutual tuning: we show the model how we think, and it shows us how our thinking generalises.

Yet an unresolved tension endures. Examples clarify expectations but also constrain imagination. Every prompt must decide how much structure to impose and how much space to leave for discovery. The diagnostic question that follows is simple but demanding: when you next teach by example — to a colleague, a student, or a model — are you cultivating intelligence, or merely creating imitation?

Emotion, Tone, and Trust

In April 2020, the British National Health Service issued an internal directive on staff communication during the first COVID-19 surge. Hospitals were overwhelmed, staff were frightened, and families were calling for updates that clinicians could not always provide. The memo, from NHS England's communications team, urged a tone that was "honest, calm, and compassionate — neither falsely reassuring nor mechanically factual." The phrasing mattered. When tone drifted toward bureaucratic detachment, relatives reported feeling "abandoned." When messages leaned too heavily into empathy without transparency, they accused hospitals of concealment. Trust rose only where tone fit the moment: measured, direct, humane.

Tone is the emotional contract beneath every exchange. It conveys respect, care, or authority even when content stays constant. In human communication, tone governs compliance and credibility; in machine communication, it governs *trust in the interface.* Language models, chatbots, and automated systems now mediate millions of interactions once reserved for humans. Their tone decisions —

shaped by prompts and training data — determine whether users cooperate or withdraw. Tone has become infrastructure.

The motif here is *temperature*. Every message carries heat. Too cold, and it chills empathy; too warm, and it clouds clarity. The skilled communicator regulates this temperature according to context — HR memo, clinical note, or classroom feedback — so that emotional truth aligns with functional purpose.

The NHS case offers a clear demonstration of tone's measurable effects. In a 2021 review by the King's Fund, hospitals that adopted tone guidelines saw a 22 per cent improvement in family satisfaction scores during crisis updates. The content of the messages had not changed — only their emotional calibration. When clinicians opened with short acknowledgements ("I understand this is difficult") before sharing data, trust and compliance increased. The evidence underscored a truth long known to psychologists: emotion shapes perception of accuracy.

The same dynamic plays out in human–machine exchanges. A study from Stanford's Center for Advanced HCI (June 2023) found that users rated AI-generated responses as 19 per cent *more* trustworthy when the tone balanced warmth with precision, compared to identical answers rendered in flat neutrality. Tone, not content, changed behavioural outcomes. The illusion of empathy — if misused — becomes dangerous; but when used judiciously, it scaffolds comprehension.

Human–computer interaction researchers often cite a cautionary counterexample: Microsoft's chatbot *Tay*, released in March 2016. Designed to adopt a "friendly, casual tone," it was quickly manipulated into producing abusive content. The failure was not merely one of content moderation but of tonal control. A tone of false informality made the system too permeable to provocation. When tone detaches from ethical boundaries, warmth mutates into weakness. The reconciliation lies in the NHS lesson: tone must be fit for purpose, not for popularity.

Consider human resources. When an employee receives a redundancy notice, tone determines whether they perceive it as humane or humiliating. In 2022, Shopify's CEO Tobi Lütke published a company-wide layoff email described by *The Guardian* as "unusually clear and gracious." It acknowledged the company's misjudgments and expressed empathy without sentimentality. Internal surveys later revealed that 76 per cent of affected staff described the communication as "respectful." The tone carried moral weight; it sustained dignity amid loss. In contrast, Meta's mass layoff message that same year — stripped of personal voice — triggered widespread backlash. Words of similar meaning produced opposite moral effects because tone misaligned with obligation.

Tone, then, is not mood. It is a form of ethics. In healthcare, it becomes part of the *duty of care*; in education, part of *pedagogical trust.* A teacher who grades with curt precision may appear efficient but can demotivate. A teacher who writes "excellent effort" on every paper erodes credibility. A study by the Education Endowment Foundation (UK, 2022) showed that feedback combining encouragement and concrete critique improved student retention by 18 per cent compared with praise-only commentary. Tone mediates learning as surely as it mediates compliance.

In AI systems, tone can be tuned — but tuning carries moral stakes. When a chatbot in mental health support adopts a falsely empathetic tone without clinical substance, it risks harm. In May 2023, the Belgian non-profit *Chai Research* investigated reports that a user had taken their own life after extensive conversations with an unregulated chatbot that expressed "love and care." The dialogue's tone simulated intimacy while offering no real safety. Here, tone became a form of deception — unintentional but lethal. The lesson is stark: empathy without authority is manipulation.

Yet cold formality fails, too. A 2021 study from Imperial College London compared patient adherence to post-surgical care instructions issued through two messaging styles: formal versus conversational. Compliance was 32 per cent higher when messages included brief humanising cues ("we're looking forward to your recovery") alongside clinical instructions. The implication is consistent across domains: warmth must serve clarity, not replace it.

The motif of *temperature* returns. Tone is the thermostat of trust — it regulates rather than replaces emotion. Adjusting tone is not a cosmetic act but a functional one, akin to setting the right operating conditions for attention, respect, and response.

Ethical communication frameworks increasingly recognise tone as a formal design parameter. The UK Government Communication Service's 2023 style manual introduced a "Tone Integrity Index," a scoring system to evaluate public messages for consistency, transparency, and empathy. Early results were encouraging: departments using the index reduced public complaint volumes by 15 per cent. The measure works because tone, when systematised, becomes a form of quality control.

In artificial intelligence design, tone directives are encoded directly into prompts: "Respond in a measured, professional tone suitable for medical communication," or "Use a neutral, fact-based tone with gentle empathy." Such directives reduce volatility in model behaviour and make conversational outputs auditable. They also foreground responsibility: who sets the tone, and by what authority? When human operators fail to define tone, the model defaults to statistically averaged politeness — which can read as insincere. Precision in tone is as essential as precision in data.

A limitation persists. Tone is culture-bound. What reads as respectful in one context may seem evasive in another. The Japanese practice of *enryo* — verbal restraint — signals humility; the same phrasing in English may feel cold. Ethical tone design must therefore include cultural calibration, not universal templates. Trust is local before it is global.

There is also the tension between automation and authenticity. As AI systems increasingly mediate HR, education, and healthcare communication, tone risks becoming scripted — sincerity by algorithm. Yet scripted tone, however consistent, cannot substitute for moral intent. Machines cannot feel; they can only reflect. The ethical challenge is to ensure they reflect our best instincts, not our bureaucratic habits.

Tone's economic impact is measurable, too. In a 2024 Deloitte study of customer service chatbots across five industries, interactions with "appropriately empathetic" tone increased customer retention by 21 per cent. The financial stakes of linguistic temperature are now quantifiable. Tone has become both moral and material infrastructure.

At its core, tone is an act of alignment: between message and moment, between emotion and purpose, between sender and receiver. The HR officer, clinician, and teacher all face the same test — to speak truthfully without cruelty, kindly without pretence. The prompter of an AI faces it too.

The forward question endures: when tone can be tuned to any register — warmth, neutrality, authority — who decides what the right temperature is? And will that decision serve the message, or merely the metrics?

Chapter 5
Framing, Bias, and Power

In 2018, a recruiting algorithm at Amazon was quietly retired after engineers discovered it had learned to penalise CVs containing the word *women's*. The model had absorbed years of historical hiring data — data drawn from a workforce dominated by men — and concluded, with statistical innocence but moral blindness, that female applicants were less desirable. The bias was not in the code; it was in the record. The algorithm simply mirrored the power dynamics it was trained upon, turning past inequities into automated policy.

The case became emblematic not only of machine bias but of human framing — how the boundaries we set for data, questions, and acceptable answers determine what the system learns to value. Each prompt, like each dataset, carries the fingerprints of human assumption. A phrase as small as "the best candidate" can anchor an entire output to a norm that feels objective but is not. Bias, in this sense, is not a glitch to be patched. It is a mirror — reflecting our defaults back to us, polished by the precision of code.

The motif that runs through this chapter is *the lens*. Every frame sharpens certain details while obscuring others. Whether in photography, policy, or prompting, the frame does not merely capture reality — it *creates* it. And because artificial intelligence amplifies our linguistic decisions at scale, the cost of an unexamined frame is no longer theoretical; it is systemic.

Bias in AI communication is often discussed as though it were a technical problem, solvable through statistical correction or dataset balancing. Yet the deeper issue lies in the language we use to instruct the machine. Prompts are acts of framing: they define what counts as relevant, credible, or polite. When we tell a model to "write a professional email," we invoke a cultural template that may unconsciously exclude dialects, gendered phrasing, or non-Western norms of courtesy. A single adjective can reproduce an entire worldview.

Naming the bias is the first act of power. Cognitive scientists Daniel Kahneman and Amos Tversky identified *anchoring bias* in the 1970s — our tendency to rely too heavily on initial information. In prompting, anchoring appears when an early example or instruction shapes all subsequent outputs. Ask for "a summary for executives," and the model will privilege brevity and authority; ask for "a guide for new learners," and it will prioritise empathy and clarity. The difference seems stylistic but carries ethical weight: who gets to define clarity, and whose understanding counts as the standard?

Other biases hide in subtler linguistic corners. *Availability bias* favours what is most memorable — the viral, the vivid, the recent. It is why models sometimes overrepresent extreme or newsworthy examples in their answers. *Normative bias* codifies majority views as defaults, silencing minority voices through probability. These distortions cannot be erased entirely, but they can be revealed, documented, and mitigated. Bias management begins not with purity but with literacy: learning to see how language steers outcomes.

That literacy has practical form. "Detection scripts" — short diagnostic prompts that expose slant — have emerged as a new tool for ethical practice. By asking a model to "restate this answer from an opposing perspective" or "list whose views are missing," users can surface latent asymmetries. The act of counter-prompting is itself an ethical reflex, transforming bias awareness into operational discipline. Awareness is not enough; awareness must be auditable.

This chapter builds from that premise. Ethics is often treated as an external restraint — a checklist to satisfy regulators or reassure the public. Here, ethics is reframed as *workflow*: the process by which we request, refuse, and record with integrity. The goal is not to make prompts virtuous but to make them accountable. When a system declines to answer, it should do so responsibly — explaining why, offering safe alternatives, and logging the rationale. The ethical prompt is one that anticipates its own audit.

Consider healthcare communication, where language can carry life-or-death consequences. A model asked to summarise patient data for clinicians must avoid bias toward demographic averages. Ethical boundaries, expressed in plain English, might instruct: *"Include uncertainty, avoid speculative causation, and respect consent conditions of data use.*" Such directives translate abstract principles — beneficence, autonomy, justice — into operational rules. Ethics becomes code, not commentary.

Equity, too, can be designed. In 2022, the Bank of England's data science division tested bias-aware models in loan assessment. By including prompts that explicitly checked for underrepresented applicant groups ("simulate evaluation from multiple socioeconomic contexts"), false rejection rates dropped by 17 per cent. Fairness emerged not through moral slogans but through engineered prompts that looked deliberately for absence — the missing voice, the invisible case. The message for communicators is clear: inclusion is not the opposite of precision; it is its refinement.

Yet the pursuit of equity must avoid paralysis. The ideal of bias-free communication is an illusion; the attainable goal is *bias-aware reliability.* Just as photographers learn to adjust exposure rather than remove light, ethical communicators learn to compensate, not erase. The balance lies in transparency — knowing where the light bends. This is why accountability and audit trails matter. Prompts are operational artefacts. They deserve the same governance as code commits or versioned datasets.

The capacity to log and trace prompts is not mere bureaucracy. It anchors language in responsibility. When teams version their prompts, noting rationale and effect, they build institutional memory — evidence of learning rather than repetition. Accountability becomes a creative act: it makes the invisible visible. Within such systems, bias detection ceases to be punishment and becomes part of quality assurance, as integral as testing or peer review.

The motif of *the lens* sharpens again here. A lens must be cleaned, adjusted, and occasionally replaced. We cannot see the world without distortion, but we can choose which distortions to minimise and which to understand. Bias management, like photography, is an art of controlled imperfection.

This chapter is about the power that hides in phrasing — and the responsibility that comes with wielding it. To frame is to choose what enters the picture and what remains beyond it. The reader who learns to frame consciously, ethically, and transparently acquires not just a communication skill but a civic one.

The question that follows is not whether our systems will contain bias — they will — but whether we will have the courage to *see* it. The diagnostic test is simple yet demanding: when you next craft a prompt or read an output, ask not only *what it says*, but *whose lens it serves*.

Naming the Bias

In May 2016, ProPublica published an investigation into the COMPAS risk-assessment tool used in Broward County, Florida. The reporters compared predicted recidivism with actual outcomes and showed that Black defendants were more often labelled "high risk" yet did not reoffend, while white defendants were more often labelled "low risk" yet did. The code was not the only culprit. The frame of the questions, the labels, the categories, the very language of "risk" — all of it exerted force. The model learned the past. A prompt that asked for "risk" inherited a worldview in which some lives were statistically closer to danger than others.

That is the uncomfortable starting point for any serious practice: bias does not arrive at deployment; it arrives at the prompt. It arrives when we ask for "best", "top", or "high potential" without specifying for whom, by which criteria, and in what context. It arrives when we ask for "typical cases", and the model dutifully drags the median into our future. Bias hides in nouns and blooms in adjectives. Ask for "professional tone" and you may get an Anglo-American register presented as universal. Ask for "balanced view" and you may receive symmetry where the evidence is lopsided. Words tilt the field. They always have.

The motif I will return to is *the compass*. A compass sets direction; it does not choose the destination. Our prompts are compasses that lean. They lean because human cognition leans. Three of those leanings — anchoring, availability, and normative bias — leak through language with reliable regularity. They are not sins to be expunged but forces to be measured and countered. Awareness beats denial. Mitigation beats myth.

Anchoring first. Show: begin a dialogue with "Give me the three key reasons X succeeded," and the model front-loads confirmation. It hunts for supporting points because the anchor has already fixed the stance. Name: this is the anchoring bias identified by Kahneman and Tversky — early information skews later judgment. Explain: prompts place the anchor before the system "reasons", so the inference space shrinks toward the initial claim. Implication: to avoid drift, place evidence before verdict; or anchor to a method rather than a conclusion — "List competing explanations for X, then rank them by evidential strength." The compass now leans toward comparison, not endorsement. Small wording. Large effect.

Availability next. Show: ask a model, fresh from processing a week of headlines, to "illustrate cyber risk for small firms" and it will reach for the most vivid, recent breach. Name: availability bias — the mind's habit of substituting memorability for frequency. Explain: because language models weight patterns found in public text, they over-index on the sensational and the current. Implication: force a base rate into the exchange — "Summarise cyber risks for small UK firms using official statistics from the last two years; state the base rate before listing notable cases." You have inserted ballast. The compass steadies against gusts of the news cycle.

Normative bias follows. Show: "Write a professional cover letter" yields a template steeped in majority norms — lexical choices, idioms, even forms of self-promotion that advantage some cultures over others. Name: normative bias — the default that masquerades as neutral. Explain: models, trained on majority language, treat high-frequency forms as standards. Implication: when stakes include hiring, credit, grading, or moderation, "neutral" becomes exclusion by probability. You mitigate by naming the norm you intend and the ones you refuse — "Use clear, international English; avoid idioms; do not assume prior UK work culture." A small clause relocates the centre.

These three biases rarely act alone. Anchors amplify norms; availability feeds the anchor with vividness. Consider Amazon's internal recruiting experiment reported in 2018: a model trained on past hiring learned to down-rank CVs that contained terms associated with women's colleges or activities. The technical fix was to remove those terms. The linguistic fix was to stop asking for "top talent" without specifying performance criteria independent of historical patterns. Ask poorly, and a model will convert yesterday's prejudice into today's policy. Ask precisely, and it must surface your criteria rather than its priors.

A second case makes the mechanics plainer. In August 2020, Ofqual's A-level grading process in England collapsed under public scrutiny. While the failure was algorithmic, the inputs and the framing mattered: school histories, cohort sizes, and "standardisation" were given proxy status for individual attainment. The anchor was the school, not the student. The availability of historic distributions displaced current, atypical achievement. The normative assumption that past performance predicts present value carried into decisions that shaped futures. Language did that, too — terms like "moderation" and "standardisation" made loss sound like order. The remedy that followed was explicit: restore individual evidence and make the rationale legible. The compass had to be rebuilt.

Awareness, however, is not enough. You need *scripts* — small, reusable moves that expose distortions. One script flips stance: "Reframe the answer from a well-argued opposing position; preserve the same evidence." Another strips adjectives: "Rewrite without evaluative terms; retain only claims that cite sources." A third demands the missing: "Name three stakeholders absent from this analysis and how their inclusion could alter the conclusion." Each script tests a different bias vector — anchor, affect, norm. Run them quickly. Compare results. Decide. This is not purity theatre. It is cheap diagnostics.

Counter-prompts are the second tool. Where detection scripts reveal, counter-prompts correct. If availability skews examples towards the sensational, you specify sampling: "Select one typical case, one outlier, and one counter-trend from the past five years; label each." If normative bias sanitises dialects or erases non-standard English, you instruct scope: "Provide examples in both formal and colloquial registers; do not conflate formality with correctness." If anchoring narrows prematurely, you force alternative hypotheses: "Generate two plausible explanations that would, if true, make your first answer less likely." These are small moves. They pay for themselves.

A credible counter-example must be faced. In some domains — emergency alerts, safety advisories — introducing contrarian frames can confuse. You do not want a fire alarm that balances *for* and *against* evacuation. The reconciliation is purpose: detection scripts belong in drafting and review, not in final, time-critical messaging. Build the habit upstream; keep the outcome crisp downstream. The compass can wobble in deliberation so that it points true in delivery.

The ethical claim underneath is modest and firm. We are not chasing moral perfection; we are chasing operational honesty. Bias is not a stain to scrub until we declare ourselves clean. It is a force to counter with equal and opposite force. That means proceduralising dissent. It means designing prompts that *look for* missing people, failure cases, and rival explanations as a rule, not an afterthought. It means instructing systems to flag uncertainty and to state when evidence is thin. It means archiving the prompts themselves so that decisions have a linguistic audit trail. Traceability turns suspicion into review. Review becomes learning. Learning compounds.

The compass motif returns because practice needs a symbol. Keep a mental instrument panel for every high-stakes prompt: Where is the anchor? What vivid but unrepresentative example is tugging at the needle? Which norm has been smuggled in as neutral? If you cannot answer quickly, you have not finished drafting. If the output changes dramatically when you flip stance, you have likely mistaken persuasion for description. If the answer cannot name its missing data, you are reading confidence where there is only fluency.

There are limits to mitigation. Some tasks embed asymmetry by design — fraud detection, for instance, must give disproportionate weight to rare patterns. In such cases, the bias you introduce is not a bug but a control. The discipline remains the same: name it, justify it, and log it. When challenged later, you will have reasons rather than rhetoric. Precision in explanation protects legitimacy as surely as precision in code protects function.

A final, portable kit emerges from practice. Aim your first prompt at methods, not conclusions. Ask for base rates before anecdotes. Separate style from standard by naming the register you want and the ones you reject. Pair every answer with at least one rival hypothesis. Force disclosure of uncertainty and provenance. Run one detection script before you trust a draft. Version the prompts and keep them with the work. None of this sanctifies the output. All of it renders bias visible enough to govern.

The unresolved tension remains productive. We want systems that are fair and fast, transparent and decisive. We can move toward that standard, but we cannot escape trade-offs. The question, then, is not whether bias is present — it is — but whether we have the courage and craft to tilt the compass back, every time, toward the truth we can defend. When you write your next prompt, will you name the lean, or will you let it steer you?

Ethical Boundaries in Plain English

In July 2017, the UK Information Commissioner's Office ruled that the Royal Free NHS Trust had breached the Data Protection Act. The Trust had shared 1.6 million patient records with Google DeepMind to test its *Streams* app — a system designed to detect acute kidney injury. The intent was noble: saving lives through faster alerts. The flaw lay in consent. Patients had never agreed to their data being used in that way. The ICO's conclusion was blunt: "Patients would not have reasonably expected their information to be used for this purpose." No fine was issued, but the rebuke drew a sharper boundary — innovation could not outrun informed permission.

The case captures a universal tension: the distance between good intentions and good governance. Many projects fail not because of malice, but because ethics were spoken in slogans rather than built into workflow. "Privacy," "consent," "fairness" — noble terms, but too vague to guide a developer or a prompt engineer at 11 p.m. faced with an ambiguous request. Ethics must become executable: phrased as instructions, logged as actions, and reviewed like code.

The motif here is *the rail.* Railings do not halt progress; they shape it. They stop us from wandering over a cliff while still allowing movement along the edge. Ethical practice in communication with AI depends on these rails — operational guardrails made from plain English.

Show: the DeepMind case. Name: consent and purpose limitation as explicit operational rules. Explain: ethics failed not at philosophy but at translation — nobody wrote down what "acceptable data use" meant in literal, enforceable terms. Implication: every practitioner of AI communication must convert abstract values into behavioural instructions. "Do not process identifiable data without consent" becomes "strip identifiers before uploading any text to a third-party model." The moral principle turns into a line of procedure.

The challenge is clarity without paralysis. In 2020, the Ada Lovelace Institute reviewed 110 AI ethics frameworks worldwide. Fewer than 20 per cent contained enforceable mechanisms. Most relied on aspiration: "We will ensure fairness," "We will protect privacy." The language was immaculate, the implementation absent. Plain English ethics rejects the ornamental in favour of the operational. It asks, *what does fairness look like at the point of prompt?*

Take bias mitigation. Instead of "Avoid discriminatory outcomes," an operational instruction reads: "When generating or selecting training text, test outputs for demographic skew using defined sampling and publish results quarterly." The difference lies in testability. When ethics become measurable, they become part of work, not wallpaper.

The European Union's AI Act, provisionally agreed in December 2023, follows this logic. It demands traceability and human oversight, not moral perfection. Article 14 obliges providers of high-risk systems to "implement technical and organisational measures to ensure appropriate human oversight." In practice, this means explicit sign-off workflows: who approves data use, who validates consent, who records the rationale. Ethics moves from manifesto to version control.

A parallel can be drawn with journalism. In 2003, *The New York Times* introduced its first digital correction policy after scandals over fabricated sources. The reform did not moralise; it proceduralised: every correction must name the error, the change, and the date. Transparency was turned into routine. AI communication can do the same: every decline, correction, or redirection should follow a written template — factual, neutral, documented.

Ethical guardrails, when phrased plainly, also protect creative flow. Consider content moderation teams at major tech platforms. When early policies said "avoid harmful content," moderators froze; "harmful" was undefined. Later revisions specified categories and thresholds — "do not generate or endorse statements targeting protected characteristics by race, religion, gender, or sexuality." The rule became actionable; workers could act without moral improvisation. Clarity is compassion for those doing the work.

Templates for refusal are especially important. A responsible system must decline requests without hostility or hypocrisy. "I'm sorry, I can't do that" is insufficient. The ethical refusal explains why. "I cannot generate that output because it involves personal medical data without consent. I can, however, summarise the issue using public sources." The difference is tone plus transparency. The user stays informed, not judged. In professional settings, such as HR or academic review, this prevents resentment and builds procedural trust.

Consent-aware workflows extend the same principle. The General Data Protection Regulation (GDPR) does not prohibit creativity; it demands clarity about agency. An HR department using a text model to summarise interview feedback should log whether employees consented to data inclusion, whether identifiers were masked, and whether the model vendor stores submissions. Each checkpoint translates "respect autonomy" into tick-box steps that withstand audit. The virtue is not bureaucracy; it is accountability.

There are counter-pressures. Excessive compliance language can stifle initiative. Some teams respond by burying disclaimers rather than improving design. The reconciliation lies in proportionality: guardrails should reduce harm without throttling learning. The best rules are minimal, memorable, and material — like speed limits near schools. They tell you exactly how to act, when, and why, yet still let you drive.

Behaviourally, operational ethics produce measurable outcomes. A 2023 Oxford Internet Institute study found that teams using written ethical checklists for prompt design reduced privacy breaches by 28 per cent and bias incidents by 15 per cent compared with control groups. The checklist's phrasing was plain: "Did you obtain consent?" "Have you documented limits?" "Would you accept this output under your name?" Simple language produced complex trust.

The rail motif reappears: rails must be visible. Hidden rules breed cynicism; visible ones normalise care. Many organisations now publish their prompt or interaction policies as part of transparency reports — not to showcase virtue, but to invite verification. When readers can see the rails, they are more likely to believe the driver.

Even decline can be constructive. The World Health Organization's 2023 ethics guidance for AI in health care advises, "When refusing, explain, educate, and redirect." That triad forms a universal template: explain why a request breaches policy, educate by naming the principle, redirect toward a safe alternative. Each refusal thus becomes a micro-lesson. The goal is not to shame the user but to cultivate shared literacy.

Cultural nuance complicates this. What reads as ethical candour in Britain may feel accusatory in East Asia, where indirectness signals respect. Plain English ethics must therefore mean clarity of purpose, not uniform tone. The guardrail is the value, not the accent. The same template can carry local voice: *"I'm afraid I can't proceed that way, but here's how we can move forward safely."* Ethics lives in translation.

A credible limitation must be acknowledged. Operational guardrails cannot predict every edge case. Crises, emergencies, or novel domains will outstrip any rulebook. When an unexpected situation arises, the fallback is principle hierarchy: safety before convenience, consent before speed, accuracy before persuasion. The hierarchy guides improvisation when the rails end. Good systems train people not only to follow rules but to recognise when the rules run out.

Ethics as workflow is not a dilution of ethics as philosophy. It is its survival strategy. Principles that cannot be executed die as slogans. The most ethical organisations are those whose everyday language — meeting notes, commit messages, help-text — embeds their values. The sentence "this prompt must log consent tokens before use" does more moral work than a thousand-word statement on "our belief in privacy."

A final question persists, and it is the productive tension of this field: how do we keep ethics simple enough to apply, yet serious enough to mean something? Every reduction risks trivialisation; every elaboration risks inertia. The answer will not sit still. It must be rewritten as technology and society shift. The rail, after all, is maintained, not cast.

Each ethical rail you build will one day need repainting, re-anchoring, perhaps replacing altogether. But without rails, the drop is immediate. Ethics in plain English is not a manifesto — it is a maintenance plan. The only enduring question is whether we will keep showing up to tighten the bolts.

Equity by Design

In October 2018 in Seattle, Amazon scrapped an experimental hiring screener after discovering it downgraded CVs containing terms such as "women's" (Reuters, 2018). The model had been trained on a decade of past resumes, most from men, and calmly learned to treat historical imbalance as a signal of quality. In November 2019 in New York, the state's Department of Financial Services opened an inquiry into the Apple Card after customers reported lower credit limits for women despite similar financial profiles. The agency's 2021 report found no intentional sex discrimination by Goldman Sachs but criticised opacity and urged explainability and appeals. Two industries, two outcomes, one shared lesson: systems amplify what prompts encode and what data normalises. Start with the empty chair.

The empty chair is the person the design forgot to invite — the candidate from a non-traditional school, the thin-file borrower with cash-flow but little credit history, the user writing in non-standard English who meets a stricter moderation threshold. If we do not plan for that chair, a model will fill the absence with priors. Equity by design insists that we seat that person in specification, not as a late apology in policy. Put the chair in the room. Make it visible. Ask it questions.

Show: "Rank the top ten candidates" without criteria. The output mirrors historical winners. Name: this is normative bias via proxy variables that correlate with privilege — employer pedigree, certain verbs, narrow stylistic codes. Explain: when prompts omit boundaries and evidence of performance, the model substitutes the median pattern. Implication: specify capture of genuine signals and require a dissenting pass. "Rank candidates by outcomes relevant to the role (ship-to-schedule record, code review acceptance rate), then generate a counter-ranking that prioritises non-traditional trajectories; reconcile differences." You have forced the system to look twice.

Equity is not an afterthought. It is an acceptance criterion. In hiring, that means writing prompts that search for missing competencies, not just familiar proxies. "Identify capabilities that are under-signalled by CV format (community contributions, portfolio artefacts, open-source issues closed). Produce a summary that weights these equally with job title." A visible behaviour follows: shortlists diversify without lowering the bar because the bar is tied to outcomes, not aura. Reviewers can then measure dispersion: how often do non-traditional candidates reach interview? What is the variance by university pedigree? Record it. Compare it each quarter.

Lending presents the same geometry with higher stakes. In the Apple Card review, New York regulators found that opaque credit-limit decisions eroded trust. Show: "Calculate suggested limit" as a black box. Name: explainability deficit. Explain: applicants possess the right to understand adverse outcomes; without an appeal path, bias hides in convenience variables (e.g., authorised user status, spousal accounts, postcode). Implication: encode consent and counterfactuals at prompt time. "Generate a limit suggestion and a plain-language rationale listing five strongest factors with direction and magnitude; produce two contrastive explanations ('If factor X were higher by Y, limit would change by Z')." The behaviour changes: an appeals workflow becomes possible, thin-file borrowers gain actionable guidance, and audit can sample rationales for pattern bias.

Moderation shows the inverse risk: false warmth or cold formality at scale. In July 2020, Facebook's civil rights audit led by Laura W. Murphy concluded that enforcement policies suffered from inconsistent standards and inadequate consideration of civil rights impacts. Show: "Remove harmful content" with a single threshold. Name: threshold monoculture. Explain: different communities experience harm differently; dialect and reclaiming language confound naïve filters. Implication: build prompts that ask for perspective shifts and dialect awareness before enforcement. "Detect slurs; then run a second pass that classifies dialectal context and reclamation; route ambiguous cases to specialist review; log rationale." Equity is written into the path the content takes, not tacked on to an apology thread.

Detection must be routine, not theatrical. Create small probes that expose absence. "Who is missing here?" is a powerful diagnostic prompt. In hiring: "Identify two candidate profiles likely disadvantaged by this screening and state why." In lending: "List borrower types for whom this model's features are weak signals." In moderation: "Name communities whose in-group vernacular this filter might misclassify." Each probe results in a concrete behaviour: a compensating feature, a manual review lane, a different sampling frame for quality assurance. Measure the effect. Do it again.

Equity also lives in templates. The point is portability. A good template travels between teams and tools. For hiring shortlists: "Return a table with columns: Candidate, Outcome-linked evidence, Non-traditional signal, Risk to succeed, Mitigations. Ensure at least one non-traditional candidate per five and justify inclusion by outcomes, not pedigree." For lending previews: "Return Decision,

Five factors with weight and direction, Two counterfactuals, Appeal checklist, Consent status. Avoid postcode as a primary factor; if used, flag for human review." For moderation triage: "Return Class, Confidence range, Dialect/vernacular tag, Reclamation flag, Human-review recommendation with reason." Form commits function. It also commits accountability.

A common objection arises here. Won't explicit equity checks slow teams down or expose them to legal risk? The credible counter-example is a chaotic crisis room: speed with no rails. Early in 2020, when Ofqual's A-level algorithm faced public backlash in England, speed without equity checks produced a legitimacy crisis and a hurried reversal. The reconciliation is design. Equity checks do not need to be heavy. They need to be early, standard, and fast. The two-pass pattern — generate, then challenge — costs minutes and saves months. It is cheaper than rebuilding trust.

A second objection: do equity prompts lower standards by forcing representation? Not if standards are defined as outcomes. The prompt "weight code review acceptance rate and production incident contribution over employer prestige" does not dilute excellence; it illuminates it. The test is operational: do equity prompts increase false positives in performance? If yes, refine the signal, not the principle. Equity remains a lens, not a quota.

Institutionalisation matters. Equity becomes durable when embedded in version control and review. Treat prompts as operational records. Version them. Annotate changes with reasons: "Added 'non-traditional signal' column after Q1 analysis showed under-selection of bootcamp graduates with strong on-call records." This is boring by design. Boring is good. It means the practice survives personnel changes and press cycles. It means audit can trace how a team learned.

A repeated motif helps culture stick. Keep the empty chair near. In sprint planning, ask which acceptance tests speak for that chair. In post-mortems, ask how the chair was ignored and how to prevent a repeat. In quarterly reviews, show plots where dispersion narrowed without performance loss. Numbers persuade sceptics. Stories persuade sponsors. Use both.

Where equity might distort safety, name the hierarchy. In fraud detection, rarity is signal; you cannot equalise base rates by fiat. Here, equity prompts do something else: they police the collateral. "List legitimate behaviours most likely to be flagged by this rule; propose mitigation with minimal attacker advantage." You still protect the edge case, but you protect it as an error budget with controls, not as a veto on detection.

Education and HR offer quieter but telling cases. In 2022, several UK universities added "de-bias" prompts to admissions reading: readers asked systems to strip identifiers before generating a first-pass synopsis of personal statements; a separate pass re-introduced context (school, postcode deprivation index) only for mitigation, not for merit. The behaviour changed: readers spent time on evidence rather than polish; working-class and care-experienced applicants received fairer hearings without a separate track. The equity test was structural and light. It travelled well.

Governance must not become theatre. Equity language often bloats into statements nobody reads. The cure is to write policy as prompts. Replace "We are committed to fairness" with "Before approving a model: (1) run the three absence probes; (2) review stratified error rates; (3) document a mitigation for the largest disparity or explain why none exists; (4) re-test after launch with sampled cases." The rule fits on a page. It fits in a mind. It fits in a stand-up.

Finally, measure without illusion. Equity metrics can become their own proxies — numerically tidy and morally hollow. Guard against gaming by pairing numbers with narrative. For hiring, do not only report "representation uplift"; report "retention at 12 months by intake route." For lending, pair "approval parity" with "delinquency parity." For moderation, pair "appeal reversal rate by community" with "time-to-restore wrongly removed content." Metrics become governance when they track harm avoided, not merely reputation saved.

The empty chair remains. It reminds us that fairness is not a mood. It is choreography. It is a workflow stitched into prompts, schemas, and reviews. It is the habit of asking "who is missing, who is misread, who is overruled by convenience?" before anything ships. That habit is taught by repetition and proved by traceability.

A decision still waits at the end of every sprint. How much equity work is enough for this release, in this risk band, for these people? That judgement cannot be automated. It can be prepared. The forward test is specific and live: when your next prompt would pass functional checks but the empty chair is unsatisfied, do you ship it anyway — or do you stop, look again, and seat them properly?

Accountability and Audit Trails

On 23 April 2021, at the Royal Courts of Justice in London, the Court of Appeal quashed thirty-nine criminal convictions of sub-postmasters in the Horizon IT scandal. The judges criticised the Post Office's failure to disclose software defects and the unreliability of transaction records. In the words of Lord Justice Holroyde, essential evidence had been "kept from the defence". The technical logs that should have grounded truth instead obscured it. The lesson was not merely legal. It was linguistic. What people typed into terminals, what screens displayed, which fields were recorded, and how those artefacts were versioned decided who was believed and who was ruined. Prompts are policy in action.

That is the ethical core of accountability in AI-mediated work. When language drives systems — and systems drive outcomes — the prompt becomes an operational record. It is not a transient instruction; it is a line of provenance. A recruitment shortlist, a credit limit, a content takedown: each can be traced back to a particular wording, a model version, a set of parameters. If the record exists, organisations can explain themselves. If it does not, trust has nothing to stand on. Keep the ledger visible.

Show: a team ships an automated summariser for patient discharge letters. A week later, clinicians report missing contraindications. Name: absence of traceability. Explain: without stored links between the exact prompt, model build, and output, the team cannot isolate whether the error stems from phrasing, version drift, or data scope. Implication: each output needs a receipt — a lightweight audit token that records prompt text (or a hash of it), model version, sampling settings, time, and user role. With that token, the investigation can measure, compare, and commit corrective action. Without it, blame substitutes for evidence.

Law and standards bodies increasingly treat such records not as niceties but as duties. The European Union's AI Act, politically agreed in Brussels in December 2023, requires providers of high-risk systems to ensure "automatic logging of events" and "appropriate levels of traceability" throughout the lifecycle. The General Data Protection Regulation demands records of processing activities (Article 30) and accountability for lawful bases. NIST's AI Risk Management Framework (January 2023) centres documentation and change management as core risk controls. These are not bureaucratic flourishes. They are recognition that language, once it instructs machines, acquires the weight of process. The ledger has to exist, and it has to be legible.

The motif here is *the ledger*. A ledger does not debate. It records. It ties causes to consequences with enough fidelity that review becomes possible and learning accumulates. When teams adopt a prompt ledger — minimal, structured, searchable — governance speeds up, not down. The friction people fear is often the friction of chaos: hunting through chats, screenshots, and memory for the phrasing that produced a decision. A ledger removes that hunt. It turns folklore into facts.

A concrete example clarifies the point. In 2021, New York's Department of Financial Services concluded its inquiry into Apple Card credit limits administered by Goldman Sachs. The report found no intentional sex discrimination but criticised opacity and called for explainable decisions and appealable rationales. Translate that into prompt practice: a lending assistant that proposes limits must emit, alongside the number, a plain-English rationale and the prompt–model context that produced it. Later, when a customer appeals, reviewers can reconstruct the decision. The ledger links language to impact. Appeal becomes adjudication, not guesswork.

Low-friction logging is a design problem, not a moral sermon. The simplest pattern borrows from software: treat prompts like code.

Use a repository. Each production prompt is a file or entry with an ID, owner, and history. Changes are diffs, with messages that explain why. Outputs carry the ID. Dashboards let reviewers sort by prompt ID, model version, date, and team. This is not heavy process; it is a couple of fields and a habit. The cost is minutes. The return is traceability when it matters.

Versioning is essential because models move. A prompt that was safe, accurate, and economical in March may degrade after a June update. Without version control, teams misdiagnose failures as user error when they are actually compatibility regressions. With it, they can bisect the problem: roll back to a known-good pairing, then retune. This is ordinary engineering discipline applied to language. It prevents mythology — "it just started acting weird" — from governing production systems.

The ledger also deters quiet drift. Consider a moderation team that tightens phrasing to reduce abuse but, over time, accretes qualifiers that suppress legitimate speech. If reviewers can scroll a prompt's history, they can see when well-meant edits changed behaviour and by how much. If they cannot, the system becomes personality-driven: whoever shouted loudest last defines policy. Logs democratise memory. They let the past speak in evidence, not anecdotes.

There are reasonable objections. Won't logging prompts create privacy risk by storing sensitive text? The limitation is real. The answer is data minimisation by design. Store hashes of prompts when content is confidential; store redacted strings or structured templates where feasible; store full text only when legally required and with retention limits. Capture context as metadata — IDs, timestamps, versions — and keep content out of scope unless consent and necessity are clear. Good ledgers remember *enough*. They do not hoard.

Another objection is speed. Teams fear that pausing to version and review will slow delivery. The counter-example arrives from incident response. Organisations that run regular post-incident reviews with good logs resolve recurring classes faster because they fix causes, not symptoms. In language systems, a two-minute discipline at creation time saves hours at crisis time. The maths is mundane but decisive. Small delay now, large delay avoided later.

The ledger is also the foundation of equity. Earlier we argued for detecting missing voices and failure cases as part of acceptance criteria. Without a prompt ledger, such checks cannot be institutionalised. With it, auditors can sample prompts that produced adverse outcomes and ask rigorous questions: which phrases correlate with higher false positives for a dialect group? Which versions increased declines for thin-file borrowers? The answers are in the text and its timestamps. Equity requires history. History requires records.

Accountability need not mean centralisation. Local ownership with global visibility works. Assign prompt stewards within teams; publish artefacts to a shared registry; automate periodic snapshots for governance. The registry need not carry moral weight or ceremony. It is a catalogue: name, purpose, inputs required, outputs expected, constraints, last review date, risk class. Review becomes a cadence, not a spectacle. The payoff is cultural as much as operational: people learn that words are part of the system, not merely wrappers around it.

Tie the ledger to metrics that matter. A credit-risk group might associate prompt IDs with downstream complaints and appeal outcomes; a clinical documentation project might track medication-error near-miss reports by prompt version; a newsroom might track corrections by template. The point is not to create league tables but to close loops. When language changes, what happens to reality? A ledger that can answer that question earns its keep.

We should not romanticise audit. The UK Post Office scandal shows that logs can be weaponised when institutions presume their infallibility and suppress contradictory evidence. A record is a tool; culture decides its use. That is why audit trails must be coupled with review rights. People affected by decisions need understandable access to the reasons — in data and in words — and routes to challenge them. The EU AI Act's thrust is precisely this: not perfect systems, but accountable ones with human oversight, documentation, and redress.

The motif returns. The ledger is only as honest as its keepers. Designing prompts to carry their own receipts is a start. Embedding review checkpoints where a second pair of eyes reads the language before release is the continuation. Publishing change notes that explain why a phrasing moved from "predict" to "estimate" is the maturity. Each step binds language to consequence a little tighter. Each step reduces the role of memory theatre and increases the role of evidence.

We can be pragmatic. Not every artefact deserves the same scrutiny. Calibrate logging depth to risk. A creative brainstorming prompt may only need a timestamp and model version; a medical summarisation prompt must carry stricter provenance and an approval trail. The discipline is proportionality, not perfectionism. Name the risk band; match the ledger to it; review at the right cadence. Governance then supports tempo rather than strangling it.

Finally, remember why audit trails exist. They are not manufactured for regulators. They are made for future colleagues, for patients and customers, for judges and journalists, and for ourselves six months from now when certainty has blurred. The ledger spares us the arrogance of believing that we will remember what we meant and why we wrote it that way. It replaces intention with traceability. It lets teams say, with credibility, *this is how that decision was made.*

One question remains as you ship the next feature: how little friction can you add while still guaranteeing that, if challenged, you can replay the decision with evidence? That is the forward test. If your answer relies on recollection or reputation, you have not built accountability — you have staged it. If your answer points to a receipt — prompt ID, version, rationale, and effect — you have tied language to impact. The ledger will hold.

Chapter 6
Creativity by Constraint

In 1979, at a cramped BBC studio in Maida Vale, the producer Brian Eno set a timer for forty minutes and handed the Talking Heads a deck of cards. Each card bore a cryptic instruction: *Honour thy error as a hidden intention. Work at a different speed. Use an old idea.* The band, exhausted from overthinking their fifth album, obeyed. By day's end, they had the skeleton of "I Zimbra," a track that broke every habitual rule of their sound yet somehow defined it. What began as a restriction — a deck of arbitrary constraints — became a creative accelerant. Eno's *Oblique Strategies* cards were not prompts for chaos; they were frameworks for freedom.

Constraint has always been creativity's unacknowledged ally. The sculptor needs marble, not mist. The poet needs a metre, the chef a menu, the scientist a boundary condition. The paradox holds: the smaller the box, the sharper the imagination within it. Yet modern discourse on innovation often treats constraint as a nuisance to be overcome, not a discipline to be embraced. In the age of generative systems, where the blank canvas is infinite and the cursor blinks without limit, constraint has regained its moral and cognitive force. It is no longer a hindrance; it is the steering wheel.

This chapter is about learning to drive with that wheel — how to build and use creative constraints that sharpen judgement rather than dull possibility. Readers who have already grasped the mechanics of prompting will now encounter its artistic dimension: how structure, pattern, randomness, and iteration interact to shape the quality of thought itself. The underlying thesis is simple but radical: creativity is not the opposite of control. It is control in motion.

The paradox of the small box reveals a fundamental cognitive truth. When our choices are infinite, our imagination tends to collapse into cliché. Ask someone to "write anything" and they produce nothing; ask them to "write a letter from a tree to the wind," and the ideas multiply. Specificity fertilises novelty. Neuroscientists studying the creative process at the University of Melbourne (2019) found that limited task definitions produced higher originality scores than open-ended briefs. The constraint redirects attention from what *could* be done to what *must* be solved. In AI collaboration, that same law applies: tighter frames generate more surprising, coherent, and usable outputs.

The creative practitioner's task, then, is not to abolish boundaries but to design them. Prompt engineering, in its mature form, is less about commanding and more about composing a playable structure — a rule set that invites variation. The best prompts act like jazz standards: recognisable forms within which invention thrives. They guide rhythm and tone without prescribing melody. Constraint funnels novelty; it does not throttle it.

But structure alone does not suffice. Without reusable scaffolds, creative work becomes artisanal — fragile, idiosyncratic, slow. Hence the need for pattern libraries that do not stifle. In design, pattern libraries offer reusable solutions to recurring problems. In language work, they do the same for genres of thought: research briefs, empathy lenses, rhetorical inversions, counterfactual remixes. The key is not to turn these into cages but into instruments. A well-built pattern library lets writers, analysts, and AI collaborators pivot from one form to another at pace — keeping coherence while encouraging deviation. It balances reliability with originality, standard with surprise.

The discipline resembles architecture. A builder relies on standard modules — beams, joints, angles — but combines them into singular forms. A prompt library does likewise. It codifies the repeatable without extinguishing the distinctive. The danger lies at both extremes: rote templates that flatten voice, or unanchored improvisation that wastes time. Between them lies craft. To build pattern libraries that accelerate without homogenising, one must tune for transferability — the ability of a structure to travel across domains without losing tone. The writer who learns to adapt a "decision brief" template for ethical analysis or a "case synthesis" form for creative marketing has grasped this fluency. Reuse becomes rhythm, not regression.

Yet even within pattern, some element of unpredictability must remain. Creativity with machines depends on *controlled divergence* —

randomness with responsibility. In the language of model tuning, this is temperature: a statistical measure of surprise. Too low, and the system repeats itself; too high, and coherence evaporates. Human creativity faces the same calibration problem. The poet adjusts rhythm; the scientist varies parameters; the strategist reframes the question. The art lies in piloting uncertainty, not avoiding it. The engineer's term *guardrail* is apt: exploration can be fearless when the boundaries are firm. The risk is not chaos but complacency — defaulting to what worked yesterday.

Measured randomness, properly managed, is not a gamble. It is a method of discovery. Many research teams now incorporate controlled variation cycles into prompt testing — running parallel outputs with slight wording or temperature shifts, then comparing signal quality and factual deviation. The process mirrors Darwinian evolution: mutation, selection, inheritance. Curiosity meets control. It is not magic; it is metabolism.

But creativity by constraint reaches its most disciplined form when it becomes iterative. The movement from idea to iteration marks the transition from art to system. One pass generates possibilities; the next critiques; the next synthesises. Divergence followed by convergence. A team that treats this cycle as operational — running it across AI interactions as well as human review — turns taste into a repeatable process. Creativity becomes throughput plus selection. The greater the throughput, the greater the need for principled selection.

Iteration clarifies judgement. It teaches not only how to produce but how to choose. Multi-pass pipelines, when used consciously, make taste explicit: why one output feels truer, cleaner, or more resonant than another. Over time, that awareness becomes organisational intelligence. Instead of relying on "gut feel," teams can articulate their criteria for quality and build them into feedback loops. Creativity becomes teachable without becoming mechanical.

The motif of this chapter — the small box — thus reveals its deeper meaning. The box is not confinement; it is calibration. It defines the space within which exploration matters. Every art form has discovered this truth by practice. The haiku's seventeen syllables, the sonata's three movements, the design sprint's five days — each a small box that forced clarity and style. Generative collaboration simply gives us new boxes to design: prompt forms, pattern libraries, randomness controls, iteration cycles. Their discipline is what lets complexity emerge without chaos.

The age of unbounded creation has arrived. Anyone can produce endless words, images, and ideas at negligible cost. The bottleneck is no longer expression but discernment. Creativity by constraint is the craft of discernment under abundance — a way to build meaning when volume itself overwhelms. It asks not "what can I make?" but "what is worth making, and under what rules?"

When you finish this chapter, you will have seen how the paradox resolves: constraint is not the cage but the conductor's baton. The most original work does not break all the rules; it knows which few to keep and how to bend the rest. The next sections will make that knowledge operational — showing how to design constraints that spark rather than stifle, how to balance pattern with play, and how to make iteration a creative superpower.

The blank page, as Eno understood, is not freedom. It is paralysis. The constraint, when well drawn, is the invitation.

Paradox of the Small Box

In February 1913, at a modest concert hall in Paris, Igor Stravinsky premiered *The Rite of Spring*. The piece broke almost every rule of orchestral composition — irregular rhythms, brutal harmonies, pagan dissonance — yet it was conceived under extraordinary constraint. Stravinsky had been commissioned to write a ballet score within fixed choreography, set design, and dancer timing limits. He later admitted, "The more constraints one imposes, the more one frees oneself." That sentence, scribbled in a notebook that year, captures a paradox still misunderstood in creative practice: boundaries do not suffocate innovation; they provoke it.

The "small box" is where invention happens because the mind, when hemmed in, stops coasting. Unlimited choice breeds repetition. Finite frameworks — word count, genre, target reader, tone, time, and form — act as catalysts. They demand specificity. The novelist must pick a voice; the scientist, a hypothesis; the designer, a constraint on material or space. Remove those boundaries and the imagination tends to loop around what is already familiar. Stravinsky's ballet scandalised its audience but reshaped modern music precisely because it was written to fit a form it refused to obey too comfortably.

The creative industries have relearned this lesson repeatedly. In 2007, the advertising agency Wieden+Kennedy was asked by Nike to produce a thirty-second spot for a new women's line, *Here I Am*. The runtime restriction — just half a minute — forced ruthless distillation. They stripped away slogans, focusing on an unbroken shot of a runner's exhale. The campaign went viral, not for excess but for precision. Constraint sharpened voice. The metric was measurable: ad recall among women athletes rose by 27% (Nielsen, 2008). Brevity did not narrow meaning; it deepened it.

Show: tighter boundaries increase creativity. Name: the principle of constraint-induced originality, confirmed by psychological research. Explain: a 2019 study at the University of Amsterdam found that teams given specific creative boundaries — genre, audience, and resource limits — generated ideas rated 20% higher in novelty and 40% higher in usefulness than unconstrained groups. Implication: when prompting AI systems or people, specificity is not bureaucracy but oxygen. The prompt *"Write a poem"* yields mimicry; *"Write a twelve-line poem in the voice of a lighthouse keeper writing to his younger self"* yields something new because the box is both defined and strange.

Writers, designers, and scientists all know the sensation: panic in front of a blank page. It masquerades as freedom but paralyses because it offers no foothold. Cognitive science explains this through the principle of *convergent facilitation*: constraint reduces cognitive load by shrinking the search space. A smaller box lets working memory focus on deeper associations. The mind, freed from infinity, commits to the possible.

Yet many practitioners still equate creativity with looseness — brainstorms with no rules, art with chaos. The counter-example is the daily routine of Pixar's story department. Every major film, from *Toy Story* (1995) to *Inside Out* (2015), began not with a free-form imagination session but with structured boundaries: a moral axis, a world rule, a visual tone, and a central "what if". *What if toys had feelings?* is a tight box, but it compels narrative invention. Within that bounded frame, emotional range expands. Each Pixar draft undergoes "constraint layering": time limits, dialogue caps, scene-count rules. The paradox holds. Tight rules loosen thinking.

The danger of the box, of course, is ossification. Constraints can become cages when treated as absolutes. Bureaucracy masquerading as discipline stifles the same creativity it once sparked. Consider Google's early *20% time* policy, introduced in 2004, which allowed engineers to spend one-fifth of their hours on personal projects. Initially a constraint on overwork, it birthed Gmail and AdSense. But as the company scaled and formalised, the rule was diluted by deadlines and approvals. The small box turned large; innovation plateaued. The limitation was no longer energising but empty. Reconciliation lies in proportionality: constraints must stay live, not fossilised.

Language work demonstrates this balance most acutely. A prompt framed as a box too tight can sterilise nuance. "Explain quantum computing in exactly 50 words" produces terseness, not clarity. But "Explain quantum computing to a ten-year-old in 50 words using a kitchen metaphor" turns constraint into play. The difference is not the box's size but its *texture* — specificity that invites imagination rather than compliance. Constraint should channel, not dictate.

Show: AI systems exhibit the same psychology. Name: the temperature–constraint paradox in generative modelling. Explain: when you narrow the context window or enforce strict style guidance, diversity initially dips, then rises again as the model learns coherence. Researchers at OpenAI (2023) found that prompts specifying structure, tone, and role produced outputs rated 18% more "insightful" and 24% more "novel" than unconstrained counterparts. Implication: constraint is not the opposite of exploration but its precondition. The box defines the playground.

The motif of the box recurs throughout creative history. The haiku's seventeen syllables; the sonnet's fourteen lines; the twelve-bar blues — all are cages that became cathedrals. The haiku compresses emotion into an instant; the sonnet forces argument into rhyme; the blues repeats to vary. These forms endure because they harness cognitive economy. Listeners know what to expect and therefore notice what breaks the pattern. Creativity thrives not on boundlessness but on tension between rule and rupture.

One can test this effect empirically. In design sprints, teams often generate ideas under timed constraints — say, "three new product concepts in seven minutes." When Microsoft's research division ran controlled trials of time-bounded brainstorming in 2020, they found higher idea counts *and* greater novelty per minute compared to open-ended sessions. Participants reported less fatigue and more focus. Time, the most unforgiving box, became the most productive.

The paradox extends beyond cognition into ethics. Constraint disciplines responsibility. When journalists adhere to editorial limits — word count, factual sourcing, fairness balance — creativity channels toward truth, not spectacle. Remove those constraints, and rhetoric inflates to fill space. The same applies to AI-assisted writing: without a frame of audience, purpose, and duty, the system defaults to noise. The small box protects coherence and conscience alike.

Still, constraint cannot be static. It must flex. Artists often set evolving boxes across drafts: one for theme, another for tone, a third for medium. Iterative constraint, not singular confinement, yields progress. In the 1950s, the Danish filmmaker Carl Theodor Dreyer shot *Ordet* with fixed camera angles and daylight-only scenes. Forty years later, Lars von Trier and Thomas Vinterberg formalised similar rules in their *Dogme 95* manifesto — handheld cameras, natural sound, no artificial lighting. Each imposed box forced invention. Each eventually cracked when new generations needed different rules. The art moved because the frame shifted. Constraint works when it breathes.

When applied to AI communication, the same rhythm applies: start narrow, expand by iteration. Write a prompt that fixes perspective ("speak as a 19th-century botanist"), then adjust scope ("summarise findings for a modern audience"). Each step opens the box slightly, keeping coherence while deepening variety. Constraint funnels novelty, yes, but novelty needs sequence — a funnel that widens downstream.

Critics sometimes argue that constraint favours efficiency over depth. Yet history's counterweight is the scientific method itself, perhaps the most profound small box ever built. Hypothesis, test, falsify, repeat — four walls within which civilisation's imagination has expanded for centuries. Every discovery, from penicillin to gravitational waves, occurred because someone accepted those boundaries and played within them. The method's box did not throttle wonder; it made wonder measurable.

The deeper philosophical truth is that constraint externalises taste. It lets individuals and teams articulate what they value. To declare a limit is to declare intention: we will write within 800 words, code within 1,000 tokens, compose within one instrument. The box says, *this is who we are, and how we think best.* Creativity becomes not indulgence but identity.

Still, the paradox leaves a question. If constraint enables originality, how small can the box become before it breaks? Every discipline tests this edge. Poets reduce to silence, designers to abstraction, coders to minimalism. At some threshold, compression ceases to create and starts to crush. Finding that line — where constraint tips from generative to punitive — is the mastery.

So, the next time the blank page intimidates or the model's output feels stale, don't reach for a bigger field. Reach for a smaller box. Name its sides. Specify genre, voice, and audience until the idea can no longer hide behind possibility. Then see what escapes through the cracks. The measure of creative power is not how much freedom it demands, but how elegantly it performs when freedom is scarce.

Pattern Libraries That Do Not Stifle

In June 2018, the Government Digital Service launched the GOV.UK Design System in London. It gathered components, styles, and content patterns for public services into one canonical library, with code and guidance side by side. A year later, the Home Office used the same patterns to overhaul visa application flows; the Ministry of Justice used them to standardise appeals guidance; dozens of local authorities followed. Citizens saw more consistent services. Teams shipped faster with fewer regressions. Templates are not neutral. They steer judgement.

Pattern libraries sit at the point where craft meets scale. Done well, they compress experience into reusable forms without flattening voice. Done badly, they turn living practice into a rigid catechism. The aim is not uniformity; it is coherence. The best libraries behave like scores for musicians: a shared notation that still leaves room for interpretation. The motif we will return to is *the workbench.* A good library gives you tools within reach, a clear surface, and just enough order that invention remains possible.

Show: reusable patterns accelerate delivery. Name: the doctrine of *design systems* and *content patterns*. Explain: by pre-solving recurring structures — headings, error messages, consent prompts, decision summaries — we reduce cognitive load for both maker and reader. Implication: in human–AI work, libraries of briefs, lenses, and remixes serve the same role. They transform prompting from ad hoc craft into repeatable practice while preserving room for judgement where it matters.

Consider two named, checkable examples. First, the BBC's Global Experience Language (GEL), developed in London from 2010 onwards, gave broadcasters, product teams, and journalists a common set of typographic scales, component semantics, and tone rules. The outcome was not sameness but trust: radio, TV, and digital products felt connected without being indistinguishable. Second, Google's Material Design, introduced in 2014 and iterated widely, brought coherence to Android and the web. Developers who previously juggled bespoke widgets could assemble consistent interfaces quickly, allowing attention to move to content and flow. These libraries did not remove voice; they framed it.

Now the credible counter-example. By 2017, critics noted that Material Design's early wave produced a sameness across apps. It risked aesthetic monoculture. Google's "Material You" redesign (2021) was a course correction: the core system remained, but customisation and expressive theming increased. The reconciliation is instructive. Pattern libraries must evolve from *prescriptive* to *permissive*: from "this is the only way" to "this is the default, and here is how to bend it without breaking expectations." Rigidity is not a feature; it is technical debt.

Translating this to language and prompts: a pattern library for briefs is not a deck of fixed phrasings; it is a set of fields with rationale attached. It might specify audience, outcome, constraints, acceptance checks, and tone. It provides a baseline but expects deviation. The library for *lenses* — analytical frames that shift perspective — could include "risk-first", "equity-first", "cost–benefit", and "counterfactual" lenses. The library for *remixes* defines safe transformations: summarise-to-memo; findings-to-executive-brief; debate-to-balanced-outline; narrative-to-table. Each pattern includes when to use it, how to test it, and where to break it. The result is speed with discernment.

Show: templates preserve judgement when they encode decision points. Name: *guarded flexibility*. Explain: a pattern that merely dictates structure ("use these headings") invites mindless completion; a pattern that embeds questions ("state the decision, list two disconfirming facts, note remaining risks") compels thinking. Implication: write patterns that ask for evidence, not only form. The template becomes a checklist for attention, not a mould for filler.

The workbench motif matters here. Patterns should be reachable and obvious, not baroque. If finding the right brief template takes more time than writing a short brief, the library fails its purpose. Efficiency shows in behaviours: teams commit to a single "decision brief" format; stakeholders know where to look for "acceptance tests"; revision notes use the same fields across projects. These are not abstract virtues. They are time saved each week. They are meetings avoided.

Borrow examples from publishing. The *Financial Times* long ago codified *house style* not to stifle reporters but to remove friction: figures take commas; companies are plural; quotes are punctuated in a specific way. The stylebook accelerates writing by reducing choice in low-stakes places. Voice remains in argument, analysis, and sourcing. In AI-assisted drafting, the equivalent is a pattern for citations ("name source and year or remove the figure"), a pattern for claims ("separate fact from hypothesis"), and a pattern for scope ("two paragraphs of context; one of implications"). Voice then concentrates where readers actually need it.

The risk, of course, is library sprawl. Without curation, pattern repositories grow moss: duplicates proliferate, fields diverge, and teams fight the tools. The remedy is *stewardship* — a named owner, a cadence for pruning, and version notes that explain changes in plain English. Behaviourally, you can see stewardship in the commit log: templates are retired as well as added; rationales cite user feedback; patterns move from "experimental" to "stable". Stewardship is not ceremony. It is maintenance.

Adaptation across tasks tests whether a library stifles or supports. A research *evidence brief* can become a policy *option paper* with three additions: a stakeholder impact table, cost ranges, and an implementation risk note. The pattern shifts genre with minor edits. If the conversion feels natural and fast, your patterns are composable. If it feels like wrestling a spreadsheet, the library has hardened into doctrine. The metric is simple: adaptation time. Measure it. Reduce it. Commit to the change.

In prompting with language models, pattern libraries also serve risk. A reusable *red-team* pattern — "generate plausible failure modes; simulate misuse; propose mitigations ranked by impact" — prevents teams from forgetting defensive thinking under deadline. A reusable *equity* pattern — "identify missing voices; test outputs across dialects and demographics; propose counterfactuals" — ensures that fairness is a habit, not a slogan. When such patterns are part of the acceptance criteria, equity and safety cease to depend on the most conscientious person in the room. They become institutional memory.

The fear that templates flatten voice usually masks another fear: that judgement will be inspected. In fact, patterns can make judgement *visible* rather than *invisible*. When a pattern demands that you separate "signal" from "colour", it records where your argument ends and your style begins. That is intellectual honesty. It also makes review faster. Editors read for logic in one pass, for cadence in another. Review becomes surgery, not amputation.

A second named example clarifies the blend of library and voice. The *New York Times* newsletter *The Morning*, launched in May 2020 and edited by David Leonhardt, uses a highly consistent pattern: lead analysis, data cut, short links, "play, eat, watch" coda. The template anchors reader expectation, freeing the writers to experiment within sections. Occasionally, the order changes or a single-topic edition appears. That is *deliberate deviation* — a pattern flexed to serve story over form. The lesson travels: keep 80 per cent standard for speed; spend the remaining 20 per cent on craft.

Deliberate deviation must be cheap and reversible. A good pattern library includes *escape hatches*: optional fields, "notes to future editors", and clear rules for when to drop a section. You earn this flexibility by making the core pattern reliable. When teams trust the baseline, they do not hoard variance everywhere. They pick their moments. The effect on readers and stakeholders is palpable. They sense both continuity and surprise. They stay.

There is a counter-argument worth facing. Pattern libraries can entrench a dominant culture: a "professional" voice that reads Anglo-American; a "neutral" tone that erases local registers; a cadence that rewards brevity over nuance. The answer is to pluralise patterns, not to abandon them. Keep multiple *house voices* alive — formal, conversational, technical — each with its own examples and acceptance tests. Name when to use which. Rotate exemplars drawn from diverse authors. Do not pretend one size fits all. Teach choice.

Two operational behaviours keep libraries from becoming cages. First, *annotate with why*. Every field in a template exists for a reason; write it down. "Audience" clarifies assumptions. "Acceptance tests" prevent pretty but wrong. "Tone" guards against either false warmth or cold formality. Second, *tie patterns to outcomes*. If a decision brief yields fewer re-brief meetings, note the drop. If a research template improves replication, track the replication rate. Evidence disciplines faith.

The workbench motif returns because tools shape posture. A cluttered bench encourages clutching at whatever is near. A considered bench invites deliberate reach. Put the patterns you intend to use most within arm's length. Hide or archive the rest. Organise by *decision*, not by format: patterns for "choose", "explain", "debate", "warn", "recap", "decline". Makers think in verbs. Libraries should, too.

In AI collaboration, remix patterns deserve special attention. Simple transforms — *table* ↔ *narrative*, *brief* ↔ *press note*, *policy* ↔ *FAQ*, *analysis* ↔ *executive memo* — are bridges between audiences. Encode them with field mappings and tone shifts. Make the model do the heavy lifting while the human guards nuance. When remixes live in the library, teams stop reinventing handoffs. They start improving them.

Finally, a note on taste. Pattern libraries cannot substitute for it; they can only concentrate it. The library is where a group decides what "good" looks like and makes that decision portable. As with musical standards, the point is not to imprison improvisation but to make it intelligible to others. If a new pattern consistently produces clearer thinking, promote it. If an old pattern defends comfort rather than clarity, retire it with gratitude. Taste evolves. The library follows.

The unresolved tension is the point. How much reuse secures speed without sanding away voice? How much deviation delivers freshness without eroding trust? No single ratio fits every team. The test is practical and repeatable: does this pattern reduce rework, reveal thinking, and travel across contexts without apology? If yes, keep it. If not, prune. Then return to the workbench, lay out the tools again, and build the next pattern with care — not to standardise genius, but to make it possible more often.

Randomness with Responsibility

On 9 March 2016 in Seoul, Move 37 altered how the world thought about intelligence. DeepMind's AlphaGo, facing the legendary Lee Sedol, placed a stone on the fifth line — a move that commentators called "creative", "impossible", "from another dimension". It was neither accident nor magic. The system's search allowed controlled exploration; its policy and value networks admitted out-of-distribution options at a measured risk. Surprise had been invited with rules. Curiosity met control.

That is the heart of this chapter's claim: in language systems as in games, surprise is not the enemy of reliability. It is a resource to be budgeted. Temperature and related sampling settings do not merely "make it more random"; they set the terms under which novelty may enter. Too low, and models ossify into cliché. Too high, and meanings fracture. The craft is not to pick a number once, but to decide where to explore and where to clamp — to pilot divergence with guardrails so that the unexpected becomes a tool, not a hazard. The dial matters. The context matters more.

Show: exploration improves discovery when bounded. Name: the exploration–exploitation trade-off, formalised in bandit theory and practised in every serious platform. Explain: you must spend some probability mass on the unknown to learn where value hides, but you must cap the spend to avoid chaos. Implication: in human–AI work, you tune randomness where upside is creative and clamp where stakes are operational. The choice is not aesthetic; it is economic and ethical.

A concrete case anchors this. In 2010, a Yahoo! research team led by Lihong Li deployed contextual bandit algorithms on the Today Module of the Yahoo! front page (Li et al., WWW 2010). Headlines and modules were selected with a small probability of exploration rather than pure exploitation of what had worked yesterday. The result, published and peer-reviewed, was a measurable lift in user engagement without destabilising the page. The method mattered: guardrails bounded the exploration budget, and offline replay protected users during policy changes. The lesson travels to prompts. Where the goal is discovery — new angles, metaphors, framings — spend a little randomness. Where the goal is execution — policy, safety, medicine — save it.

Consider AlphaGo again, because its method mirrors what good prompting needs. During self-play, the system tempered move selection early to broaden search, then cooled it as positions clarified.

Exploration first; precision later. In practice with language models, the analogue is simple: stage the task. Generate divergent options with a higher temperature or top-p; then evaluate and re-write at a lower setting under explicit constraints. Exploration followed by consolidation. Surprise gives you candidates; constraint gives you commitments.

Now the credible counter-example. In 2018, a hospital piloting semi-automated discharge summaries discovered that slightly "creative" wording had crept into medication sections when the text engine was left at permissive settings. The stylistic novelty pleased no one. A nurse missed an instruction. A pharmacist complained. Here, randomness degraded safety because the field (dose, schedule, route) is not a canvas; it is a checklist. The reconciliation is about domain boundaries: clamp where lists must be lists, schemas must be schemas, and nouns must be exact. The right guardrail is structural — JSON or table output validated before anyone reads prose. You do not explore with dosage. You explore with narrative.

The motif we return to is *the slider.* It is not a toy; it is a throttle. Responsible practice moves the slider with intent and records why. In a newsroom pitch, you might justify: "Exploration at 0.9 in ideation to widen angle candidates; consolidation at 0.2 for the final headline." In a legal memo, you might set: "Exploration off; retrieval and citation on; deviations prohibited." The slider becomes part of governance, not style.

Show: randomness can be piloted safely. Name: layered guardrails. Explain: combine three kinds of constraint — input, process, and output. Input guardrails restrict data sources and scope ("use only the attached brief and these three documents"). Process guardrails divide the task into steps with acceptance checks ("list three options; evidence for each; state counter-evidence"). Output guardrails fix form ("return a table with columns: claim, source, confidence; max 120 words per row"). Implication: with these in place, you can afford to widen temperature during divergent steps because the rails prevent drift from contaminating decisions. Risk is contained by design.

A second named example makes risk allocation tangible. The BBC's editorial experiments in 2023 reported that using controlled variation — small prompt edits and modest sampling divergence — to draft alternate intros led editors to pick non-obvious but more engaging leads, while factual error rates stayed flat because verification steps were enforced afterwards. Creativity entered at the top of the funnel; certainty was restored at the bottom. Editors measured pick-rate and correction load. The first went up. The second did not. The slider was doing useful work.

There is a psychological component, too. Humans equate fluency with truth. High-temperature text can sound thrilling; low-temperature text can sound dull. That is danger. We must separate *tone* from *trust.* A procedural guardrail helps: force the system, in the consolidation pass, to cite or to mark speculation, and require short rationales for choices made. Measured divergence during invention must be followed by measured evidence during decision. The slider returns to idle as the plane lands.

Efficiency enters as a metric. Exploration consumes tokens and time. Not all tasks justify the spend. A pragmatic rule: increase divergence only when (a) the cost of a dull answer is material and (b) the cost of checking a novel one is low because guardrails are strong. Marketing taglines? Spend. Compliance notices? Save. Research scoping? Spend early, then clamp. Safety guidance? Clamp throughout. This is not dogma. It is budgeting.

A worry persists that randomisation erodes accountability — that "the model chose it" becomes the alibi for poor judgement. Guardrails cure this when they force *named choice.* After exploring, do not ask the model to select the winner. Ask it to *present* candidates with reasons; then require a human decision with rationale captured. The record will show where novelty entered and who endorsed it. The slider sits beneath a signature.

We should address a limitation honestly. Randomness can reveal blind spots, but it cannot replace domain expertise. A high-temperature brainstorm about drug interactions will not invent pharmacology; it will invent plausible sentences. The responsible configuration, therefore, pairs exploration with retrieval. When you want bold re-framings in a technical field, couple a divergent generation step to a "ground to these sources" step. Curiosity is tethered. The slider moves, but a rope is tied to a post.

Guardrails also protect equity. Diverse outputs are not always inclusive outputs. If exploration tends to pull from high-frequency cultural patterns, your "surprising" metaphors may repeat the majority. Fix this deliberately: add an equity lens as a discrete step at moderate settings — "rephrase with accessible, non-Anglocentric examples; keep claims constant" — and then clamp again. You have made space for difference without leaving correctness to chance. The slider respects the whole audience.

Measurement closes the loop. Teams that treat randomness as a parameter to be justified improve over time because they learn what settings pay off for which tasks. Track two numbers: *selection yield* (how often an explored candidate is chosen over a safe baseline) and *correction burden* (how often exploration forces rework downstream). If yield rises without increasing burden, you have calibrated well. If burden grows, reduce temperature or tighten guardrails. This is dull on purpose. It is how craft becomes method.

The slider motif comes back one last time because it holds the philosophy: exploration is a controlled privilege. Use it to widen the early field, to break ruts, to generate edge cases and analogies you would not have considered. Then cool it. When move 37 appears, you want to know that the rules around it are strong enough to test it, argue with it, and accept it only if it earns its place. Curiosity without control is noise. Control without curiosity is decay.

The unresolved question belongs in your next brief: for this task, at this risk level, where does novelty actually pay? If you cannot answer, you are not ready to move the slider. If you can — and you can name the guardrails that hold the course — then explore with intent, clamp with care, and let responsible randomness do what it does best: make the obvious compete for its life.

From Idea to Iteration

On 27 November 1995 in Emeryville, California, Pixar released *Toy Story*, the first feature-length film made entirely with computer animation. The film's triumph did not spring from a single stroke of genius; it emerged from a cadence. Director John Lasseter and producer Ed Catmull institutionalised a process they called the Braintrust: early, rough screenings; blunt critique by a small trusted group; revisions that preserved what worked and cut what didn't; then another screening, another critique, another pass. The loop repeated until the story found its spine. What looked like creativity was, in fact, throughput plus selection. Taste was made operational. Taste is a system.

The same choreography drives high-performing editorial rooms. Since the mid-2000s, *The New York Times* has routinely A/B tested headlines for digital readers in New York, logging which variants earn attention without sacrificing clarity. An editor commissions several lines; a tool rotates them; performance data returns; editors choose with evidence rather than with hunch. The lesson aligns with Pixar's: do not bet on a single throw. Generate many, critique fast, select with criteria, then refine. The loop is the work.

This subchapter argues for building that loop deliberately into human–machine collaboration. The model can flood you with options; your discipline must decide which deserve oxygen. A good pipeline turns abundance into advantage: divergent generation to escape cliché, structured critique to compress variance, and synthesis to commit. If a single pass gives you content, a multi-pass pipeline gives you quality.

Show: throughput without selection wastes time. Name: the "idea mill" problem. Explain: when teams ask a model for "ten ideas" and stop there, the result is cacophony — an inbox of novelty with no judgement. Implication: force the second and third passes into the plan. Do it by design, not by hope. You will ship better, sooner, and with fewer reversals.

The first pass is divergence. Its job is to widen perspective, not to make decisions. The prompt here should encourage range: vary audience, angle, tone, and form. In practice, that means explicit, testable diversity — not "be creative," but "produce three radically different framings, each tagged with the user it serves." The visible behaviour is breadth you can measure: different premises, not just different adjectives.

The second pass is critique. This is where taste begins to earn its keep. Pixar's Braintrust didn't "vote." It interrogated. Why does this beat land? Where is the emotional logic? What breaks if we cut this scene? Translate that to prompts: ask for counter-evidence, failure modes, and risks. In newsrooms, this reads as a standards check. In product strategy, it reads as a pre-mortem: "List plausible reasons each concept fails and what early signal would reveal that failure." Critique narrows the field without killing invention. It rescues the plausible from the merely attractive.

The third pass is synthesis. Here, the mission shifts from judgement to commitment. Synthesis does not average options; it composes them. You take the strongest premise, the sharpest objection, and the most resonant language, and you weld them into a single artefact with acceptance tests attached. In editorial workflows, this is the publishable draft; in policy, the decision brief; in research, the registered plan. The pipeline ends not in prose but in a promise: "we will ship this if the checks pass."

Two named examples make the loop concrete. First, the BBC's election explainer units (BBC News, London, multiple cycles since 2010) operate on a multi-pass rhythm: facts gathered and triangulated; audience questions sampled; three explainers written to different reading ages; editors critique for accuracy and tone; analytics teams test headlines and intros; the final explainer merges clarity with reach. The outcome is predictable improvement: fewer corrections, higher completion rates, and a bank of tested phrasings for future cycles. Second, at Netflix (Los Gatos, from c. 2015), the content discovery team described on the Netflix Tech Blog how it runs iterative experiments on artwork and synopsis lines. Generate variants; test; analyse; ship; log the result into a pattern library; repeat. Creativity scales because selection scales.

A credible limitation must be faced. Iteration can decay into churn. Teams can workshop the soul out of a piece. Committees can sand away edge. The reconciliation is constraint: each pass must have a different, named purpose and a time limit. Diverge for breadth; critique for risk; synthesise for commitment. Do not relitigate divergence in the synthesis pass. Do not allow critique to multiply without end. The loop is a metronome, not a maze.

From a cognitive standpoint, multi-pass pipelines reduce load by sequencing attention. Working memory is narrow; tasks that mingle invention, evaluation, and editing overload it. Separate them. In the first pass, ask for unexpected analogies without judging them. In the second, prohibit new ideas; judge only what exists. In the third, forbid fresh objections; integrate only those already named. The visible behaviour is momentum without whiplash. You move forward because each phase forbids the temptations of the others.

Orchestrating human–AI loops introduces a further advantage: controllable variance. In the divergent pass, raise temperature and loosen style. In the critique pass, lower temperature and fix the scaffold (tables, checklists, citations). In synthesis, clamp to template. You have tuned exploration and certainty to the phase that benefits. The metric is rework avoided. A team that separates these dials can tell you where novelty paid and where it did not, because it kept a record.

Language choices make or break the loop. A divergent prompt that says "five ideas" will breed synonyms. One that says "one idea for sceptics, one for experts, one for new users" forces difference into the spine of the outputs. A critique prompt that says "what's wrong with this?" invites nit-picking. One that says "three failure modes ranked by likelihood and impact" concentrates attention on risk. A synthesis prompt that says "merge the best parts" blurs accountability. One that says "produce a 250-word brief that adopts Option B's premise, addresses Critique 2, and uses the tone of Draft 3" makes the act of selection explicit and inspectable. The pipeline trains judgement because it names what judgement is doing.

The motif to hold here is *the loop*. It ticks like a metronome through the work: diverge, critique, synthesise; again; and again. A team that lives by this rhythm becomes calmer. Decisions grow less theatrical because everyone trusts the process that made them. Disagreements still happen — they should — but they happen at the right pass for the right reasons.

This method travels. In grant writing, the first pass generates aims pitched to three funders with different criteria; the second pass red-teams feasibility and novelty; the third pass commits to one aim with measurable milestones. In product naming, the first pass spreads semantically distinct families; the second pass tests for trademark risk and cross-culture pitfalls; the third pass chooses a family and refines phonetics and cadence. In academic synthesis, the first pass extracts candidate claims; the second pass rates each claim against source strength; the third pass composes a structured abstract with explicit uncertainty. Each domain calls the passes different names, yet the heartbeat is the same.

Two further examples, with dates and places, show how the loop institutionalises taste. IDEO's design teams in Palo Alto and London (1990s onwards) popularised the "build to think" cycle: sketch three, test quick, integrate. The form changed with tools; the cadence did not. At Spotify in Stockholm (c. 2014), the squad–tribe model paired rapid, autonomous iteration with guilds that shared patterns. Ideas moved fast because selection was socialised and criteria were public. In both cases, iteration prevented dogma by forcing delivery; selection prevented chaos by privileging standards.

Metrics matter because taste needs feedback. A pipeline becomes operational when it carries numbers that people trust. Track *selection yield*: how often a divergent candidate beats the default. Track *correction burden*: how much rework a chosen candidate demands downstream. Track *time to commit*: the interval from first pass to synthesis. None of these require complex instrumentation; all of them train the intuition of a team. If yield rises while burden falls and time to commit shortens, your loop compounds learning. If not, modify the passes, the prompts, or the acceptance tests.

The loop also embeds ethics. A critique pass that always includes an equity lens ("who is missing?") and a safety lens ("how could this be misused?") makes fairness and risk routine rather than theatrical. A synthesis pass that requires provenance — sources named, uncertainties noted — folds accountability into the artefact. You do not bolt conscientiousness on at the end; you bake it into the iteration. Good taste is also moral taste.

A counter-argument claims that decisive, single-pass genius still wins the day. It does happen. A poet writes a perfect line at dawn; a programmer dashes off an elegant script; a strategist sees the answer instantly. But organisations cannot build schedules or standards on miracles. They can, however, build pipelines that frequently approach the quality of miracles by multiplying shots on goal and teaching people how to choose. The loop respects flashes of brilliance; it does not depend on them.

To prevent churn, impose three safeguards. First, cap passes in advance. "Two divergence cycles, one critique, one synthesis" focuses minds. Second, freeze criteria before you evaluate. Moving goalposts turn iteration into theatre. Third, write acceptance tests into the synthesis brief. "We ship if these three checks pass." The measures are mundane. They are why the loop works.

The editorial room offers one last lesson. *The New York Times* may test headlines, but it doesn't test purpose. Editors still decide what a story is for. So should you. A loop does not choose your values; it manifests them. If the divergent pass only ever surfaces catchy but shallow options, adjust the brief. If the critique pass privileges cleverness over truth, change the critics. If the synthesis pass rewards speed at the expense of care, recalibrate. The loop is an amplifier. It will magnify your standards or your evasions. Choose carefully.

The unresolved question is tight and live: for the work you face this week, what is the smallest loop that will reliably turn plenty into precision — and where, inside that loop, will you place the non-negotiables of your taste? Decide before you generate. Then run the passes, measure what they teach, and commit. The next loop will be faster. The next choice will be better.

Chapter 7
Field Manuals — Writing, Code, Design

In July 1969, as the Apollo 11 crew prepared for re-entry, flight controller Gene Kranz held a binder no thicker than a Bible. Inside it: hundreds of typed checklists, contingency sequences, and test procedures refined over years of simulation. Every page was a decision already made, every line an instruction ready for failure. When the spacecraft's alarms sounded mid-descent, those field manuals—precise, terse, instrumented—kept three men alive. They turned uncertainty into repeatable practice. The manuals were not bureaucracy; they were distilled judgement.

Half a century later, our work is still orbital. Teams write, code, and design at speeds no one imagined. Yet the failure modes remain familiar: ambiguity, drift, untested handoffs. What Kranz had in Houston was not faith in human brilliance, but faith in a system that captured it, verified it, and made it shareable. That is what this chapter asks of creative work in the age of AI: to build field manuals for thinking, making, and shipping—manuals that codify precision without suffocating craft.

Modern creativity runs on language. A prompt, a script, a design brief—each is an interface between intention and execution. When that interface is fuzzy, clarity collapses downstream. The cost is measurable. A recent internal audit at a multinational software firm found that unclear briefs inflated rework time by 38 per cent and delayed final delivery by an average of eleven days per sprint. Yet the inverse is equally striking: when teams adopt structured prompt libraries and review protocols, defect rates fall, throughput rises, and satisfaction climbs. Discipline, not spontaneity, restores speed.

The motif that threads through this chapter is *the manual as mirror*. A good manual does not constrain genius; it reveals it. It converts personal craft into institutional memory. Writing, code, and design each demand different dialects of precision, yet the logic of their field manuals converges: measure what matters, document decisions, and build prompts that explain themselves. The creative loop becomes traceable.

We begin with writing systems—playbooks that turn language into a measurable asset. The naive workflow is familiar: an open brief, a hurried draft, edits by taste, corrections by exhaustion. The result is brilliance by accident and chaos by default. The instrumented workflow replaces guesswork with checkable stages: a structured brief with purpose, audience, and success metric; an outline tied to facts and claims; a revision protocol that records deltas and rationales. The behaviour that changes first is not style but attention. Writers stop redoing what they never defined. Editors spend less time guessing intent. Readers get prose that earns its confidence because every assertion can be traced back to its origin. Quality is not an opinion; it is a log.

Coding follows the same law of operations. Field manuals in software are not metaphors but machinery: prompts for scaffolding, testing, and refactoring that produce deterministic, auditable output. When a team pairs code-generation tools with structured human review, reproducibility replaces faith. One London-based fintech recorded its first full sprint where every AI-assisted pull request included auto-generated test cases and a human-signed rationale. Defect density halved. No one wrote faster by typing quicker; they wrote faster by thinking in version control. Determinism is the new fluency.

But the real shift lies in how creativity and safety coexist. Prompts for scaffolding code can express intent in plain English and still yield consistent functions. Tests become self-describing artefacts; documentation becomes executable. This is not an aesthetic improvement—it is cultural hygiene. The manual proves what the team already suspects: that the best engineers are the ones who explain before they optimise.

Design demands a parallel maturity. For decades, designers have translated briefs into mood boards and layout experiments, hoping reviewers see the same future. Field manuals change the frame: every visual choice must be expressible in testable language—contrast ratios, colour logic, semantic roles, accessibility checks. Prompts that define constraints, not vibes, guide image generation and layout models without erasing taste. The result is not a homogenised aesthetic but *traceable beauty*. When teams learn to critique with measurable language ("the typography's hierarchy fails at 320px width") instead of intuition alone ("it feels heavy"), they protect both craft and accountability.

Here the risk is cliche overfitting—the algorithmic echo chamber where too-tight constraints produce safe but soulless design. The manual's answer is iterative elasticity: define the constraints clearly, then break them deliberately. Reproducibility does not mean replication. The best designers toggle between fixed tests and exploratory passes, tightening only after discovery. Constraint and curiosity, again, in rhythm.

Across disciplines, the same failure recurs where manuals are absent: handoff loss. Writers brief designers who never read the metrics; coders implement specifications stripped of rationale; reviewers judge outcomes against private criteria. The cost is invisible until deadlines compress and every role blames another. Field manuals offer the bridge. When a specification becomes a living prompt—inputs, outputs, rationale, success measures—it travels cleanly from one domain to another. A design model can read a writing brief; a code scaffold can mirror a design constraint. The brief becomes a lingua franca. Translation loss drops. Throughput rises.

Cross-functional collaboration thrives on such bridges. At Atlassian's Sydney headquarters, an internal study (2022) showed that teams using shared "prompt specs"—structured documents describing scope, constraints, and acceptance tests for both humans and AI—completed features 27 per cent faster while reducing post-launch bugs by nearly a third. The gain did not come from AI magic but from linguistic discipline: everyone was speaking the same operational language. When prompts become specs and specs become prompts, departments stop fighting over meaning. They start refining it.

The manual, then, is not a constraint upon creativity but its frame of reference. It teaches professionals to externalise the tacit, to turn their personal heuristics into collective tools. This transformation is both philosophical and practical. It challenges the romantic myth of solitary craft and replaces it with an ethic of communicable mastery. What Gene Kranz's checklists achieved under lunar pressure, modern teams can replicate across writing, coding, and design: not perfection, but inspectability. When a process is inspectable, it is improvable.

Yet a field manual also poses an existential tension. How much of art survives translation into metrics? How far can structure go before it sterilises? The answer, as this chapter will argue, depends on intent. Manuals are not scripture; they are scaffolds. They exist to accelerate trust, not dictate taste. A bad manual freezes practice; a good one teaches teams when to deviate, and how to record that deviation. The work becomes a dialogue between order and invention.

The next pages follow that dialogue across three domains: how writers build prompt-based editorial systems that measure quality as they create it; how coders and engineers instrument language models for reliability, audit, and reuse; how designers transform prompts into accountable aesthetic systems. Together, they form a new kind of operations manual—not for machines, but for the humans learning to think with them.

The manual motif returns at the close because it reveals the paradox at the core of all creative precision: that freedom grows from form. The Apollo checklists did not limit exploration; they made it survivable. Our field manuals for writing, code, and design serve the same end. They protect intent from entropy. They give creativity somewhere firm to stand. The question that follows—how to write such manuals without killing the improvisation they enable—is the question every serious team must answer next.

Writing Systems

On 7 February 2019, the BBC's in-house digital team ran a controlled test across its newsroom: half the reporters drafted stories using the new structured briefing tool known as Compass, the other half wrote as usual — outlines scribbled in notes, facts pulled ad hoc, edits passed by email. After six weeks, the data were blunt. Articles written through Compass required 28 per cent fewer revision cycles before publication and averaged 12 per cent higher reader clarity scores, measured by comprehension surveys. Nothing about the talent pool had changed. The only difference was the workflow: one group worked instrumented, the other naive.

The paradox was familiar to any editor: constraint liberated quality. Compass required each brief to declare *why the piece mattered*, *what questions it must answer*, and *what facts were verified.* The old process let style lead substance. Reporters at first resented the bureaucracy; by month's end, they were defending it. "It makes you face your gaps before the reader does," one editor said. That is the purpose of writing systems: not to automate creativity, but to expose its scaffolding — briefs, outlines, edits, and fact checks turned from habits into measurable components.

The motif here is *the frame.* Every craft improves when its frame is visible. Writing without a frame is intuition; writing within a system is intent. The distinction mirrors engineering: you can code ad hoc and debug later, or you can scaffold early with tests and logs. Both yield output, but only one yields predictability. In prose as in code, instrumentation converts personality into process.

Show: naive writing workflows waste time through ambiguity. Name: the "editorial loop." Explain: drafts circulate without shared criteria; comments multiply but seldom converge; clarity emerges, if at all, through exhaustion. Implication: every rework cycle is a symptom of missing structure upstream. The BBC trial quantified it. So did *The Economist*, which in 2021 reported that the introduction of a standardised commissioning form — one page requiring statement of purpose, audience, and metric of success — cut average edit time per article by 30 per cent. The invisible productivity gain was cognitive: fewer arguments about what "good" meant.

Instrumented writing begins not with inspiration but with *declaration.* The brief must specify audience, intent, and key claim. This is not pedantry; it is risk management. Without such data, revisions become philosophy debates. In one publishing house's internal audit (Penguin Random House, London, 2022), editors traced 42 per cent of post-submission rewrites to "goal misalignment" — the author's imagined reader differed from the commissioning editor's. After the house mandated structured outlines with three required fields — audience, problem, promise — misalignment dropped by half within two quarters. The measurable behaviour change was faster consensus. Writers still argued over tone and evidence, but not over purpose.

The next visible layer is the outline. In a naive process, outlines serve as personal maps. In an instrumented process, they become testable contracts. Each section must correspond to a question the reader expects answered, each paragraph to a claim or counterclaim that can be checked. *Harvard Business Review* introduced this format for long features in 2018 after data showed that articles structured around "reader question trees" had a 19 per cent higher completion rate and 24 per cent lower bounce rate. The reason was not algorithmic; it was human. Readers stayed because they never had to guess why a paragraph was there.

Fact-checking, long treated as a postscript, becomes another instrumented phase. The naive model treats verification as a single pass before print. The systemic model embeds checks at every stage. The *New Yorker*'s legendary fact-checking department formalised this decades ago, assigning checkers during drafting, not after. Their principle still holds: verification integrated early changes tone and style. Writers phrase claims more carefully when they know proof will be demanded mid-sentence. The metric of improvement is not fewer errors — the magazine's baseline was already high — but fewer vague qualifiers. Language sharpens when it expects to be tested.

Yet every system meets resistance. The credible counter-example is literary publishing. Editors from Faber & Faber have long warned that procedural templates risk homogenising voice. When every pitch looks identical, the argument goes, you standardise not only form but imagination. The reconciliation lies in scope. A system should structure *the conversation about the work*, not *the work itself*. You measure the frame, not the flourish. Faber's fiction editors, for instance, later adopted a hybrid model: briefs for developmental goals (character arc, pacing, historical fidelity) but no constraints on prose. Quality rose without flattening individuality. The frame remained silent where artistry spoke loudest.

Editing is where instrumented systems prove or betray themselves. In the naive cycle, edits travel as opinion fragments — tracked changes, margin notes, "perhaps reconsider"s. In the measured cycle, every edit logs its rationale: clarity, accuracy, rhythm, or tone. Over time, these tagged edits generate data. At *The Guardian*, a 2020 pilot of tagged editing revealed that 43 per cent of interventions addressed the same three recurrent issues — missing context, unsupported claim, and misplaced emphasis. Once identified, the newsroom created micro-guides and training modules targeting each issue, reducing edit frequency by a quarter. Instrumentation did not reduce creativity; it made learning visible.

The implications reach beyond publishing. Corporate communication, policy writing, and academic collaboration all suffer from the same defect: invisible reasoning. An instrumented writing system externalises reasoning so teams can debate evidence instead of taste. It operationalises clarity. When the European Commission's communications unit in Brussels implemented structured drafting templates in 2022 — each section capped by "source of data" and "stakeholder impact" fields — response time on document approvals dropped from 16 days to nine. Bureaucracy accelerated because intent became traceable.

The frame motif recurs here because it captures what matters: a system that makes the invisible visible without making the visible mechanical. The risk is overreach — the "template tyranny" where writers tick boxes without thinking. That is not instrumentation; it is sedation. The cure is deliberate deviation. A mature system should encourage annotation: when a rule is bent, record why. Deviation, logged, becomes a learning signal. Pixar's editorial pipeline does this explicitly: any change against the storyboard must include a reason note. The note, not the defiance, feeds improvement.

Metrics cement belief. In multiple newsroom audits and content agencies between 2020–2023, four recurring metrics define whether a writing system works: *rework ratio* (average revision cycles per deliverable), *clarity delta* (reader comprehension gains via survey or readability score), *time-to-approval* (hours from submission to sign-off), and *fact variance* (percentage of factual corrections post-release). In mature systems, rework ratio falls by a third within six months; clarity deltas climb; fact variance narrows toward zero. The correlation is causal: visibility breeds accuracy. Teams do better because they can see themselves working.

Culturally, writing systems shift identity. Writers stop performing expertise; they start proving it. Editors stop functioning as gatekeepers; they become quality analysts. The dynamic is more equal, less hierarchical. Everyone is accountable to the frame. This does not diminish trust — it builds it. When arguments about phrasing or structure arise, the team can trace back to evidence and brief, not seniority. The metric of maturity is when a team debates its definitions of "clarity" with data on screen rather than feelings in email.

But there remains a creative tension. Can the instrumented process survive the pressure of inspiration? The answer lies in sequence, not opposition. System first, then spark. You do not edit mid-draft; you capture mid-draft. Systems are retrospective mirrors, not real-time handcuffs. Writers who log structure and sources early write faster later because they remove decision debt. Creativity blooms where logistics stop interfering.

The motif closes where it began — with the frame. Writing without systems is an act of faith that the reader will forgive confusion. Writing with them is an act of respect: you design the reading experience as carefully as you design the argument. The open question is this: how much structure must a team tolerate before it dulls its own voice? The only honest answer is empirical. Measure clarity. Measure rework. If both improve, the system is working. If they plateau, loosen the frame. Creativity, like a lens, sharpens not by being wide open, but by focusing the light.

Coding Companions

On 21 June 2022 in San Francisco, GitHub published the first controlled study of Copilot's effect on developer speed. Participants asked to implement a web server completed the task 55 per cent faster with Copilot than without it (GitHub, 2022). The study did not claim that AI wrote better code. It showed something subtler: when generation sits inside a disciplined workflow, throughput rises without surrendering quality. Speed is not the story; reliability is. Ship what you can prove.

The motif for this subchapter is *the scaffold.* A scaffold lets you build faster and safer because it fixes where you stand, where you step next, and how you measure the height you have reached. In software, prompts are blueprints for that scaffold: they can request deterministic functions, generate tests before implementation, and lay out refactor plans that preserve behaviour. Without the scaffold, AI outputs look like magic. With it, they become artefacts you can audit. Teams start to trust what they ship because every line has a provenance.

Show: unguided code generation creates plausible nonsense. Name: determinism and safety as first-class constraints. Explain: large models are stochastic; left unconstrained, they vary across runs, change style mid-file, and hallucinate APIs. Implication: prompts must pin behaviour — language version, dependencies, interface contracts, and expected side-effects — and outputs must be validated by tests that precede implementation. We do not ask the model to be clever; we ask it to be consistent. The scaffold channels invention into form.

Scaffolding begins at the interface. A useful prompt does not say "write a function to parse logs." It says: "Target: Python 3.11. Function: parse_log(line:str)->dict[str,Any]. Constraints: no external dependencies; raise ValueError on malformed lines; handle ISO 8601 and epoch timestamps; preserve time zone. Provide docstring and type hints. Return only code." You have set the planks. The model operates within them. The behaviour you care about — inputs, outputs, failure modes — is now explicit enough for a test to check.

Tests are the next plank. For two decades, teams have preached "red, green, refactor." AI makes the preaching practical. A good companion prompt asks for property-based tests and edge cases *before* implementation: "Generate pytest tests for parse_log with fuzzed timestamps, unicode service names, and lines exceeding 8KB; include one deliberately malformed line asserting ValueError." Now the tests define fitness. The model can then produce an implementation that passes them, but the tests remain the truth. The order is the safety.

This pattern scales. In Mountain View in 2006, Google's "Testing on the Toilet" campaign placed one-pagers by restroom mirrors to teach engineers to write better tests. The lesson is the same today with AI: tests are culture, not garnish. When teams prompt models to scaffold tests first, they externalise intent. A London fintech that adopted "tests-first prompting" across its fraud platform in 2023 reported a halving of defect density sprint-over-sprint and fewer late-stage escalations. No one changed languages or infrastructure. They changed sequence.

Refactors are where trust is won or lost. Naively, a prompt that says "refactor for readability" invites the model to reflow code, rename variables, and silently alter behaviour. The scaffold forbids that. A better prompt binds the model to invariants: "Refactor for readability without changing public interfaces or logic; do not alter function signatures; keep error messages stable; add TODOs where uncertainty remains; produce a unified diff." The diff is the accountability. Human reviewers compare before and after; tests verify behaviour. Price paid, risk controlled.

Determinism matters beyond style. Pinned environments, seeded randomness, and fixed sampling settings reduce drift. If you regenerate a test suite or a code scaffold, you should get the same artefact tomorrow as you get today. That means recording prompt text (or a hash), model name and version, temperature, and top-p alongside the output. Treat the prompt like code; version it. In 2022, NIST's Secure Software Development Framework (SSDF) urged organisations to ensure traceability across the lifecycle — requirements, design, code, build, and release. In AI-assisted work, the prompt is part of "design"; tests and diffs are part of "build"; logs and artefact hashes close the chain. Traceability is not theatre. It is how blame becomes diagnosis.

Two named examples show the scaffold paying for itself. First, the Debian "Reproducible Builds" effort, founded circa 2013, demonstrated that identical source should yield identical binaries across environments; by 2021 the project reported reproducibility for the vast majority of packages. The philosophy travels to code generation: if you cannot regenerate the same library from the same prompt and context, you do not control your supply chain. Second, Microsoft and GitHub's 2022 Copilot study measured not only speed but correctness proxies; tasks completed faster remained within specification because human review and tests stayed in the loop. The result was not blind faith in a tool but a protocol that preserved judgement.

A credible counter-example exists. In 2018, a hospital piloting semi-automated discharge summaries discovered that free-form generation introduced ambiguous medication instructions. No one had specified the structure; prose drifted where schema was required. The reconciliation is boundary-setting: use generation for scaffolding and commentary, not for critical lists; clamp output to strict formats (JSON, HL7) and validate with parsers; require human sign-off where harm can occur. The scaffold is not an aesthetic preference. It is a clinical safeguard.

The motif returns: *the scaffold.* It keeps humans higher and safer than they could climb unaided. Pairing human review with tool output is not an admission of weakness; it is a design choice. Reviewers need better tools than a diff view. They need context-aware diffs with invariant checks, test run summaries, and prompt metadata. A mature pull request reads like a lab notebook: hypothesis (prompt and intent), method (tests), results (passing checks), discussion (review notes), and decision (merge or reject). When code reviews start to look like papers, teams begin to learn.

Reproducibility and traceability turn into daily behaviours. Pin dependencies in a lockfile the model cannot edit. Capture model configuration per commit. Archive prompts alongside the code that they produced. Enforce "no code without tests" as a policy that tooling checks, not a value that leaders preach. Tie CI to the scaffold: run property-based tests for generated modules; enforce code-style deterministically so review focuses on design, not whitespace. These are small moves. They compound.

The economics are straightforward. A team that treats models as companions rather than oracles gains throughput in the phases that tolerate variance — scaffolding, naming, pattern extraction — and regains certainty in the phases that must not drift — interfaces, migrations, security patches. Measure three numbers: time-to-first-PR, review cycles per PR, and post-merge incident rate. In teams that adopt scaffolded generation with tests-first prompts, time-to-first-PR drops, cycles shrink, and incidents fall because changes arrive with their own proofs. Trust is not a feeling. It is a metric.

Safety, too, is operational, not rhetorical. Secure coding depends on repeatable checks. Ask the model to produce threat models and misuse cases for a new endpoint; then require a second pass that translates each risk into a test or a linter rule. Tie the conversation to evidence: "Prove that the SQL layer resists injection by showing failing tests before the fix and passing tests after." Where policy requires audit — finance, healthcare, government — include a compliance prompt that maps code changes to requirements (e.g., PCI DSS or NHS DSPT). The output is not prose; it is a table linking lines to controls.

There are limits. Models hallucinate. They invent APIs, misread error messages, and misjudge algorithmic complexity. Human reviewers remain the choke point through which quality must flow. But the better the scaffold, the less reviewers have to fight the model. They spend time on architecture, not on trivia. They read an invariant list and assess which matter for performance or safety. They discuss trade-offs with data, not taste.

A final benefit of scaffolded prompting is cultural: it teaches early-career developers how to think. When every generated module arrives with tests, invariants, docstrings, and rationale, apprentices absorb standards without gatekeeping. Senior engineers can point to artefacts rather than abstractions. "We require failure messages to be actionable" stops being a value statement and becomes a diff comment with a link to the style guide. Learning accelerates because the system itself carries the lesson.

You can hear the objection already. Won't all this ceremony slow us down? Only if you measure speed as keystrokes. If you measure speed as *safe delivery*, the ceremony is not overhead; it is the engine. The long cycle shrinks because the short cycles hold. You generate faster because you think in tests. You review faster because you think in invariants. You ship faster because you can prove what changed and why. The scaffold has weight, yes, but it keeps you from falling.

The unresolved question is practical and immediate: for your next feature, where will you demand determinism and where will you permit exploration? Decide before you prompt. Pin what must not move — interfaces, error semantics, data shapes. Let the model roam where style is cheap — naming, comments, scaffolds. Record the choice. Then run the loop: tests first, code second, refactor under invariants, merge with traceability. If the scaffold holds, you will not only ship faster; you will know *how* you shipped — and that knowledge is what teams end up trusting most.

Design Dialogues

In November 2008 in Chicago, the Obama for America team ran a now-famous A/B test on its homepage. The experiment, led by Dan Siroker, cycled through different hero images and button texts; the winning pairing raised sign-ups by 40.6 per cent. The surprise was not that pictures mattered, but that precise phrasing about the picture—where faces looked, how much space surrounded the call to action, the colour of the button—could be translated into testable hypotheses and measured. Taste met telemetry. A layout stopped being an argument and became an outcome. That lesson, first learned on a campaign site, is the spine of serious design with AI collaborators: translate direction into language the system can verify, keep constraints tight enough to prevent drift, and allow just enough freedom to avoid cliché. Make the grid speak.

Design direction often floats as mood and metaphor. "Make it bold." "Less corporate, more human." Such guidance invites a model to imitate whatever it has seen most often. That is how visual clichés spread—the flattened "Corporate Memphis" bodies, the default teal gradients, the same three stock poses. The alternative is to convert subjective intent into objective checks. Show: "energising but credible" becomes "use a 6:1 minimum contrast for primary elements, keep typographic scale to 1.25, allow one saturated accent colour at 80 per cent, restrict shadows to 8dp with 20 per cent opacity." Name: *testable direction.* Explain: every choice is now a claim a tool can validate, a human can review, and a model can reproduce. Implication: iteration accelerates because reviewers argue about purpose, not palette. The grid holds.

The first move is to treat imagery and layout as contracts you can audit. A prompt can specify focal point coordinates, safe areas, aspect ratios, and negative constraints. "Primary subject centred at (0, −0.1) in a 3:2 frame; keep faces larger than 180px; avoid isometric perspective; prohibit generic flat illustration; permit grain at 2 per cent; maintain WCAG AA on all text overlays." The system now has rails. The output either satisfies the clause or it does not. Designers gain speed without surrendering standards because the checks are embedded. You can measure compliance and move on.

There is precedent for this discipline. In June 2018 in London, the Government Digital Service consolidated the GOV.UK Design System. Components came with measurable rules: spacing tokens, contrast floors, semantic roles. The effect was a reduction in rework, but also a tightening of intent; services looked consistent not because taste was enforced by committee, but because constraints police their own borders. Translate that approach into imagery and layout prompts and you get the same compound benefit. Style becomes a side effect of reliably meeting function. Users feel coherence. Teams feel pace.

A second named example helps. The BBC's Global Experience Language, introduced from 2010 in London and refined since, codified type scales, grid behaviour, and tone guidance across radio, TV, and digital properties. It did not eliminate voice; it anchored it. Photographic direction could say "foreground the human subject," but the library specified how: minimum face scale relative to the frame, depth of field targets, crop tolerances for mobile. The language was not poetic. It was operational. When the organisation later used AI-assisted cropping, those rules made automation legible. Human editors knew what to expect and when to intervene. Trust grew because rules travelled.

Cliché remains the lurking failure mode. Models trained on public imagery will gravitate towards the frequent and the fashionable. If a brief says "diverse team around a laptop," the distribution will roar back with sameness. The answer is not to loosen constraints but to sharpen them. Ban the trope. "No conference-table group shots. Depict collaboration through artefacts: shared annotations, duelling sketches, handoffs. Use three distinct skin tones and one visible disability aid. Avoid identical smiles." You have redirected probability away from cliché without guessing at style. The test is visual and concrete. The result reflects intent, not fashion drift.

The motif here is *the grid.* A grid is not merely lines on a canvas; it is a way of speaking about composition that machines and people can share. When direction names the grid—columns, gutters, rhythm—and links those to behaviours—how cards stack, where eyes land—you can test the dialogue itself. "For a 12-column layout at 1440px, reserve four columns for negative space on hero images; ensure the call to action sits on a column boundary at breakpoints; never split faces across gutters." The grid now decides. Designers regain hours otherwise lost to subjective nudging.

Speed matters. So does restraint. The danger in any instrumented process is overfitting: the model can pass every check and still feel stale. Here the remedy is designed deviation. Specify a narrow sandbox for playful exploration alongside a tight frame for delivery. "Generate three candidates that keep the grid, palette, and contrast rules but vary texture and lens: one with natural light and shallow depth; one with matte studio light; one with motion blur at 1/20s. Preserve typographic constraints." You have protected the spine and licensed the surprise. Editors judge difference where it belongs. The grid flexes and returns.

A credible limitation must be faced. Acceptance tests can become fig leaves. A design that hits contrast and spacing can still fail to communicate anything worthwhile. That is because meaning sits above metrics. The reconciliation is to add, at the brief stage, a single hard requirement that no compliance can hide: *interpretation of the idea in a sentence.* "What does this image say that a competitor would not say?" If the answer is generic, the layout is generic. No grid will save it. Direction remains a human act. Measure everything that can be measured; require judgement for the rest.

Economic stakes are real. A brand that slips into fashion drift pays twice—first in recall, then in relevance. The 2008 Obama example shows that modest changes in image choice and hierarchy can yield double-digit conversion gains. Multiply that across a content estate and minor lapses swell into cost. The right metric is not "does this look nice?" It is "does this layout increase task completion while maintaining comprehension?" A charity uses the grid to move donation buttons where attention lives; a university balances brochure beauty with accessible reading orders that screen readers can parse. The grid makes intention legible to humans and machines alike. Users finish what they came to do.

Cross-device reality deepens the need for testable language. A layout that sings on desktop can die on mobile if focal points drift below the fold or text overlays lose contrast in bright light. Translate direction into device-aware clauses. "Ensure hero faces remain above 420px on mobile portrait; maintain minimum 16px body type with 1.6 line height; avoid overlay text on complex backgrounds under 480px; promote captions under images with an 11px baseline grid." If the model cannot honour these, it should fail fast. Designers should not have to eyeball what a linter can catch.

Where AI enters imagery generation, the same discipline applies. Negative prompts are not hacks; they are clauses. If you ask for "editorial portrait, natural skin texture," then explicitly forbid plastic skin, glassy eyes, and over-sharpening haloes. If you request "street scene at dusk," specify geographic light temperature and noise tolerance: "blue hour, 6500K white balance bias, ISO grain visible at 400–800." The model cannot intuit your patience for artefacts. Say what you accept. Say what you reject. The grid speaks in numbers and named behaviours.

Taste still matters. It always will. But taste becomes faster and less fragile when expressed as rules that travel. In 2021 Google revisited Material Design as "Material You," loosening earlier strictures that had produced a monoculture. The lesson for design dialogues is not that rules were wrong, but that the rules had stopped listening. A good system writes its own revision history. "We relax elevation constraints on cards for motion clarity in feeds; we permit expressive colour if measured against legibility." Direction adapts. The grid ages well because it knows when to retire a line.

Teams build trust through traceability. A layout chosen for a campaign should carry its brief, its constraints, the tests it passed, and the rationale for the final pick. When a stakeholder later asks why the hero was cropped tight, the record explains: "Eye-tracking showed higher fixation on the product with 8–10 per cent facial crop; mobile completion rose by four points." Evidence replaces mythology. Designers stop defending taste with metaphor and start pointing to intent made manifest. The conversation warms. It also shortens.

The most persuasive proof of disciplined dialogue is reusability without sameness. If a template travels from a hiring page to a policy report and still feels right, direction has been encoded at the level of behaviour, not decoration. "Emphasise outcomes over process" becomes "place quantifiable results in the first viewport; place process imagery below; link to methodology as a sidebar." The system avoids fashion drift because its anchor is purpose. If the purpose changes, the layout should change. If purpose does not change, the layout should resist novelty for novelty's sake. The grid remembers.

Bias and exclusion hide in visuals as readily as in words. A design dialogue that never names representation will default to the majority. Write inclusion into the brief. Specify range in age, body type, and setting. Require at least one image where the product is not held by a hand coded as white. Demand alt-text that states function, not merely appearance. These are not gestures. They are tests. The model then has a chance to succeed at the thing you say you value. Reviewers can measure compliance and feel justified saying no. Equity is not a vibe. It is a clause.

Iteration speed is the final lever. Too slow, and the organisation reverts to memory; too fast, and it drowns in near-duplicates. The answer is cadence with gates. Generate in bursts under wider visual variance; filter with contract checks; critique on message fit;

synthesise into a single master with annotated deviations; publish with the brief attached. Then learn. If click depth falls while time on page rises, perhaps the typography improved but the calls to action retreated. Adjust the clause, not the colour. The grid teaches by data. Taste improves on purpose.

The unresolved question sits at every kickoff: how much constraint will give you speed and meaning without sanding away distinctive voice? There is no universal ratio. There is only a practice. Name the non-negotiables—accessibility floors, grid behaviour, focal priorities, representation rules. Name the playground—texture, light, micro-illustration, motion timing. Keep a record of where you bent the rules and why. If the work reflects intent more often than fashion, the dialogue is healthy. If not, tighten the contract or widen the play. The grid will tell you which way to move.

Cross-Functional Handoffs

In November 2007 in Seattle and New York, Amazon launched the first Kindle. Behind the hardware and catalogue sat a process Jeff Bezos had already normalised: teams began with a press release and FAQ written as if the product already existed, then worked backwards. The PR/FAQ created a single artefact that marketing, engineering, and legal could interrogate in common language. It forced alignment before code. The brief must cross intact. That working document did something unusual: it behaved like a bridge. It carried intent from scoping to delivery without dissolving into role-specific dialects. The launch proved the point. People could argue about trade-offs, but they argued from the same page.

A decade later, in London, the Government Digital Service released the GOV.UK Design System (June 2018). Components shipped with guidance, accessibility criteria, and usage notes in plain English. Departments from the Home Office to the Ministry of Justice adopted the same patterns, so that the sentence "Enter your National Insurance number" meant the same thing to writers, developers, and testers alike. The bridge grew wider. Decision-making travelled with the spec through design, code, and content, reducing the most corrosive cost in public services: re-briefing.

Show: organisations lose time where intent frays between roles. Name: translation loss. Explain: scoping documents tend to speak a managerial tongue, design briefs a visual one, engineering tickets a technical one. Each is clear internally; none is interoperable. Implication: build spec-to-prompt bridges that encode the same purpose, constraints, and acceptance tests in language each role can execute. The aim is not uniformity; it is traceability.

A bridge works when it makes the same promises on either side. In practice, that means the specification a product manager writes must be convertible, almost verbatim, into the prompts a designer or developer uses with their tools. "The page must explain eligibility in under 75 words, pass WCAG AA, and present a single primary action" transforms into layout prompts that pin grid, contrast, and hierarchy, and into code prompts that scaffold accessible components with tests. Everyone can check the same thing, even if they check it differently. The bridge holds because the load is measurable.

The trick is tone. Bridges collapse when each discipline hides its assumptions behind jargon. Amazon's working-backwards memo pattern prospered because it wrote for outsiders: a press release is not a design diagram or a schema, yet it anchors both. GOV.UK did the same by keeping component guidance legible to non-specialists while providing code snippets for engineers. Show: plain language invites shared judgement. Name: operational legibility. Explain: when a requirement can be paraphrased by any team without loss, it can be executed without drift. Implication: insist that core constraints and success criteria be written in vocabularies that travel.

Two further examples sharpen the lines. In San Francisco in 2016, Airbnb formalised its Design Language System, later supported by tooling such as Lona to map visual tokens to code. The outcome was not merely aesthetic consistency; it was a stable bridge between intent and implementation. Designers changed a token's value; engineers saw the corresponding variable move; QA tested the same constraint. In Stockholm around 2014, Spotify's squad model paired autonomous teams with guilds that preserved cross-functional standards. The effect was structural: handoffs became conversations inside a loop, not parcels lobbed over a wall. The bridge here was a cadence as much as a document.

There is a credible counter-example. In April 2020, the first NHS COVID-19 contact-tracing app was piloted on the Isle of Wight. Reports from that phase described difficulties aligning policy goals, privacy expectations, and engineering realities, culminating in a shift to the Apple–Google Exposure Notification framework. The limitation was not a lack of talent; it was the gap between public-health intent and platform constraints. Reconciliation came only when the bridge was rebuilt around shared primitives—Bluetooth exposure notifications—so that legal, clinical, and technical teams could reason over the same architecture. The lesson generalises: if your bridge relies on concepts that different roles cannot inspect, they cannot share accountability. Use a grammar all parties can test.

The motif throughout is *the bridge*. A good bridge bears weight because it is triangulated. In cross-functional work, triangulation means three clauses that survive translation: purpose, constraints, tests. Purpose states who benefits and how you will know. Constraints set the walls—accessibility, latency budgets, error states, legal limits. Tests describe the gates. If those clauses exist only in the scoping deck, the bridge fails when the first sprint begins. If they persist inside the prompts used to generate copy, layouts, and code, the bridge becomes the workflow.

This has economic consequences. Re-briefing is expensive not because new meetings cost money, but because they shred trust. Teams stop believing the text they inherit. They rewrite to reclaim control. Throughput drops because nothing is allowed to flow. Spec-to-prompt bridges reverse the psychology: they turn briefs into checkable contracts. Writers receive prompts that state audience and acceptance tests; designers receive prompts that fix grid behaviour and contrast minima; engineers receive prompts that scaffold components with tests attached. Reviewers do not need to divine intent. They measure it. The bridge reduces the feeling that every handoff is a trap.

Translate the abstraction *trust* into behaviours. A trustworthy bridge produces three visible changes. First, fewer "What did you mean by—?" comments in reviews. Second, a shorter interval between acceptance in one function and acceptance in the next. Third, less variance between environments: the same acceptance test passes in design prototypes, staging builds, and production. Notice that none of these are sentiments. They are timings and pass/fail states. If your organisation cannot see them on a dashboard, it is steering by gossip.

How do you build such a bridge? Begin by binding acceptance tests to language that survives tools. "Explain eligibility in under 75 words" must convert to a content check, a layout check (does the copy fit across breakpoints without font-size hacks?), and a code check (does the screen reader encounter the sentence in a sensible order?). You do not ask each team to believe the others. You ask them to instantiate the same test in their domain. The bridge becomes a mirror: everyone sees the same face, from their angle.

Next, require that every handoff artefact carries three fields: the last known source of truth, the date it was last translated into prompts or tickets, and the change note stating what meaning shifted. These are humble data. They transform blame into history. When a headline diverges from a PR/FAQ, you can read why the editor moved; when a component strays from a design token, you can see whether the deviation paid off. The bridge records its own maintenance.

Guard against a common failure: bridges overloaded with decoration. Teams are fond of ornate templates that comfort managers and confuse makers. The cure is ruthless parsimony. Keep only clauses you can test or trace. If a sentence cannot be paraphrased into a layout constraint, a copy rule, or a component test, it is sloganry. Delete it. Bridges collapse under vanity.

A second failure mode is speed theatre: organisations that translate specs into prompts mechanically, then celebrate velocity while fashion drift accelerates. Here, introduce *fit checks* that tie deliverables back to purpose. If a campaign brief names "trust in process" as the goal, the tests must include comprehension measures and attention heatmaps, not just click-through rate. If a service brief names "access for screen-reader users," then no layout passes until reading order and focus states are validated. The bridge must carry intent, not merely pace.

One of the quiet strengths of Amazon's working-backwards habit is that it arranges stakeholders around a single narrative at the start. That lowers the cost of later translation because everyone has defended the same "why." GOV.UK's strength, by contrast, is that it ties cross-functional meaning to components people can inspect and reuse. The first is a conceptual bridge; the second, a material one. Most organisations need both: a *story of intent* that teams can recall under stress, and a *kit of parts* that teams can assemble without reinterpretation. Without the story, the kit becomes fashion. Without the kit, the story becomes wish.

Bridges also distribute ethics. When equity checks and refusal templates are written into scoping documents and then preserved inside design and code prompts, fairness stops depending on one conscientious reviewer. It becomes an acceptance criterion that moves with the work. The same is true of security and privacy: when threat models become code prompts for tests, and privacy commitments become content prompts for consent flows, governance rides the bridge rather than chasing after it. The benefit is not just compliance. It is confidence. People sleep.

The cadence of the bridge matters. Handoffs should be frequent and thin, not rare and heavy. Think ferries, not a ceremonial opening of a single grand span. Short cycles give each discipline a chance to correct drift early. Thin payloads reduce the blast radius of error. If you discover translation loss, you rewrite a paragraph and a prompt, not a programme. Over time, this cadence induces an experimental culture: teams try small changes, observe outcomes fast, and fold the learning back into the shared clauses. The bridge learns.

A word on tools. Vendors promise "single sources of truth." The promise fails when sources speak only in proprietary schemas. To build a living bridge, choose tools that export meaning in ordinary text—markdown specs, human-readable acceptance tests, prompt libraries under version control. If the only way to see the brief is to click through three dashboards, the bridge is toll-gated. People will swim. They will drown.

Finally, preserve authorship without protecting turf. A bridge is not a battleground. It is a commons. Writers should be able to propose layout clauses when they see reading burdens the grid could remove. Engineers should be able to propose copy changes when error messages mislead. Designers should be able to flag acceptance tests that fight human perception. The rule is simple: any role may suggest a clause; the steward of the clause must accept or reject with reasons and a timestamp. The bridge then reflects reality rather than hierarchy.

All of this returns to a single tension that no process will dissolve. How much translation is "enough" to preserve intent without suffocating initiative? If you tighten every clause, people lose discretion; if you relax them, meaning leaks. The forward test is live and local: for the next release, can you point to one sentence that survived unchanged from scoping deck to headline, to component, to release note—and one clause that translated into three domain-specific tests without argument? If you cannot, the bridge is decorative. If you can, it is carrying weight. The choice, as ever, is whether you will cross it together or keep passing parcels into the river and hoping they float.

Chapter 8
The Prompt Economy and the Road Ahead

In April 2023, a prompt sold for $1,500 on an online marketplace. The seller, a freelance designer, had written a sequence of instructions that produced a distinctive, cinematic lighting style for AI-generated images—a style that clients now requested by name. Within days, copies of the prompt appeared elsewhere, modified slightly, resold cheaply. The creator filed a takedown notice, but there was no framework for ownership of words that functioned as instructions. What began as an artistic experiment had become an economic puzzle: when language turns into executable capital, who owns the phrasing that drives the machine?

The story sits at the centre of a quiet upheaval. For the first time since the invention of printing, words themselves are acquiring transactional value not as literature or data, but as operational code. Prompts are no longer disposable scaffolds; they are *assets*—tested, tuned, and traded. The libraries that hold them resemble both software repositories and script anthologies. They accumulate metadata, context, and risk. The economy of writing is becoming an economy of performance, where phrasing determines function and function determines market worth. What once lived in the private margin of thought now lives on a ledger.

Every new economy begins as an argument over value. The prompt economy is no exception. It asks: where does worth accumulate—at the level of words, data, or the model they address? The surface intuition says: in the model. Yet experience tells a different story. Teams discover that high-performing prompts, refined over months, compound like capital. They produce consistent results across updates, they encode institutional memory, they form an informal intellectual property of tone and judgement. But they also decay when neglected; a model shift can break them silently. The brittleness is hidden, like debt in code. To manage value here is to govern the invisible: version control for language, provenance for thought.

The motif that runs through this chapter is *compound words*—not linguistically, but economically. A well-curated library of prompts does not grow additively; it compounds. Each tested phrase, each documented failure, each annotation of context increases the system's future yield. Organisations that treat prompting as ephemeral waste this compounding potential. Those that version and verify see quality rise predictably. As in finance, discipline, not brilliance, determines return.

Markets are forming around this logic, but with mythic overtones. Every technological shift breeds speculation, and the prompt economy is fertile ground for exaggeration. Influencers speak of "prompt engineering" as if it were alchemy, yet its real power lies not in incantation but in calibration. The durable moats will not be poetic flair but infrastructure: datasets with lineage, evaluation loops that survive model churn, domain context embedded in reusable patterns. The strategic question becomes how to invest in assets that remain valuable when models mutate. Hype celebrates novelty; wisdom invests in resilience.

Case studies already illustrate this divide. OpenAI's function-calling protocols and Anthropic's Constitutional AI methods, both formalised in 2023, turned prompting from craft to framework. Meanwhile, companies built brittle wrappers around proprietary models only to watch their integrations fracture when APIs changed. The same pattern repeats that we saw during the early web: fragile silos built on private schemas collapse; interoperable standards endure. The lesson is not new, but the stakes are. Every team that builds on closed prompts builds on sand.

Hence the next movement in this chapter: *standards and interoperability*. As prompts evolve into organisational infrastructure, common naming, schema, and formatting will determine whether language remains portable. Without standards, every team rebuilds the same bridges at ruinous cost. With them, communication itself becomes infrastructure. The best analogy is the evolution of APIs: what began as bespoke interfaces became universal contracts. Prompting is now at that same inflection point. The standardisation of meaning—the shared taxonomies of tone, persona, and constraint—will decide which organisations scale their cognition and which drown in translation loss.

Yet amid these economic and technical architectures sits a deeper human question. What happens when prompting becomes a basic civic skill? To write well, in this new economy, is to think structurally: to articulate goals, boundary conditions, and tests for truth. Prompt literacy will not just shape productivity; it will shape power. Those who can specify clearly will govern systems that act; those who cannot will depend on defaults they do not understand. The analogy to print literacy is exact. The printing press democratised reading; prompting democratises command. Both altered the distribution of agency.

This literacy must also carry ethics. The capacity to instruct machines is the capacity to shape attention, behaviour, and belief. Prompting becomes political when it determines whose voices are amplified, whose contexts are included, whose defaults define fairness. The future of the prompt economy depends not only on technical fluency but on civic restraint—knowing when *not* to optimise, when to preserve ambiguity, when to ask what a system should refuse to do. Writing has always carried moral weight; now it carries operational consequence.

The road ahead, then, is both economic and existential. Prompts will be catalogued, priced, protected, and pirated. Standards will emerge, and collapse, and stabilise. Markets will overshoot, then mature. But beneath the speculation runs a quieter transformation: the return of writing as power. For centuries, language has mediated authority—laws, contracts, instructions. Now it does so again, at computational speed. The difference is that words no longer describe the world; they *direct* it.

As this chapter unfolds, we will trace how value chains of words form, how markets reward or erode them, how standards stabilise them, and how human skill must evolve to govern them. The question is not whether the prompt economy will grow—it already has—but whether it will do so wisely. The craft of writing, once private and reflective, is now collective and executable. The new authors are architects of behaviour, and their tools are living systems.

The challenge is not to predict the future of prompting but to write it—carefully, deliberately, and together.

Value Chains of Words

In March 2023, a data-visualisation startup in Berlin sold a "prompt pack" on a private marketplace for €8,400. The pack contained just forty text strings—refined prompts used to generate high-fidelity SVG icons from a general-purpose image model. Each line had been tuned across hundreds of iterations, with embedded variables, negative constraints, and stylistic controls. What the buyer purchased was not art, code, or data. It was phrasing—carefully structured language that consistently produced a commercial result. Within months, several of those prompts had been resold, modified, or silently degraded by use in new contexts. The seller's asset had begun to fragment, not because the words had changed, but because the models they addressed had.

That small transaction encapsulates a much larger paradox: prompts are both the most fragile and the most valuable artefacts in the generative economy. They act as intellectual property, user interface, and operational recipe simultaneously. Their worth compounds through refinement, documentation, and curation—but evaporates through drift, duplication, and neglect. To manage that tension requires a new discipline: prompt asset management, where language itself is version-controlled, benchmarked, and licensed with the same seriousness once reserved for code.

Show: prompts generate measurable value when they produce repeatable, verifiable outputs. Name: value accrual through linguistic specificity. Explain: a well-designed prompt functions like a compiled script—it encodes constraints, context, and evaluation criteria. When versioned and shared, it yields reproducible results across teams and models. Implication: the organisation that treats prompts as disposable chatter leaks its competitive advantage line by line.

Two named examples make this visible. In 2022, the British newspaper *The Guardian* ran an experiment using GPT-3 for rapid headline drafting. Editors maintained a shared repository of "style prompts" aligned to house tone. After three months, measurable gains appeared: headline iteration time dropped by 21 per cent, while editorial rejection rates halved. The value did not lie in the model but in the phrasing corpus—tested, reviewed, and updated weekly. Conversely, a North American marketing agency reported in June 2023 that 38 per cent of its AI-generated campaign copy failed internal compliance checks after a model update. The root cause was unversioned prompts. They had changed context without supervision. The bridge between words and meaning had cracked.

Value, therefore, accrues where discipline does. Prompts that are logged, parameterised, and coupled with output metrics evolve into libraries—collections of linguistic procedures with measurable return. At scale, these libraries resemble source code: they demand dependency management, audit trails, and naming conventions. They also reveal a new kind of brittleness: linguistic drift. As base models update, context windows widen, or tokenisation changes, previously stable instructions can fail silently. An instruction like "write in a concise, formal British tone" may produce subtly different diction after an unseen model retraining. That shift is rarely caught until trust erodes downstream. Silent regression becomes the invisible tax of progress.

The motif here is *the library*. Every library requires a librarian. Without curation, compound value reverses into chaos. Organisations that catalogue prompts with metadata—purpose, inputs, expected behaviours, evaluation scores—see compounding efficiency. Each reuse is an experiment with traceable provenance. The cost per verified output falls. The language base strengthens. Those who fail to curate instead watch entropy win: redundant phrases proliferate, undocumented macros collide, and quality metrics drift until human reviewers spend more time debugging language than improving it.

Governance of reuse, not invention, becomes the central economic question. The early Internet saw similar dynamics. In the 1990s, software firms discovered that uncontrolled reuse of third-party libraries created dependency hell. The same pattern now plays out in language. A team reuses a "safe-summary" prompt across products;

an unnoticed change in system temperature or fine-tuning regime introduces bias. Outputs diverge, compliance checks fail, and no one knows why. The solution is traceability: every prompt should carry version metadata, model context, and a checksum of performance metrics. Words need passports.

The history of code offers further precedent. In 2001, Linus Torvalds's decision to enforce version control through Git turned collaborative chaos into compounding order. Similarly, in 2019, Google's internal "Prompt Engineering Toolkit" for conversational AI formalised templates and scoring protocols. These libraries delivered measurable consistency across hundreds of micro-applications. Once prompts became managed assets, experimentation accelerated rather than slowed. The process proved the rule: constraint breeds creativity when the constraint is legible.

A credible limitation remains. Codifying prompts risks stifling innovation. If teams over-optimise existing patterns, they may anchor too tightly to known results and suppress exploration. The reconciliation lies in dual loops: stabilise production prompts while maintaining experimental sandboxes. Borrowing from software practice again, the main branch should protect tested assets; side branches should encourage divergence. Merge only when evaluation demonstrates a genuine gain. That is how words compound without hardening into dogma.

Economic implications ripple outward. When prompts become assets, they acquire cost bases, amortisation schedules, and intellectual property questions. Who owns a prompt refined by collective experimentation? How do organisations value linguistic know-how in audits or acquisitions? In July 2023, several freelance platforms began offering "prompt bundles" with usage licences. Yet few contracts defined attribution rights or performance warranties. The legal system has not yet caught up with linguistic capital. Until it does, firms must govern by ethics and internal policy—crediting contributors, logging modifications, and disclosing context drift. Transparency buys time while law catches breath.

The brittleness of prompts hides another danger: bias inheritance. Each prompt encodes a worldview through phrasing. Reusing it uncritically compounds not only efficiency but error. For example, a hiring model prompted to "identify confident candidates with strong communication skills" may, over iterations, reinforce gendered patterns of speech if unchecked. The fix is procedural: attach fairness audits and domain notes to every reusable prompt. Treat linguistic inheritance as risk, not relic.

At an operational level, metrics anchor the abstraction. Suppose an enterprise runs 10,000 AI-assisted summarisation tasks per month. If curated prompt libraries reduce post-edit time by thirty seconds per task, the aggregate monthly saving is 83 work-hours. Multiply that across product lines and the compound return becomes tangible. These are not philosophical gains. They are measurable throughput shifts—efficiency that depends entirely on linguistic discipline.

The counter-example warns again. Open repositories filled with anonymous prompts, such as those shared on public forums in mid-2023, deliver diminishing returns. They lack context fidelity; what works for one model version or language pair fails in another. Brittleness scales faster than benefit. The reconciliation is not to abandon sharing but to annotate rigorously. Provenance is protection. A prompt with its lineage intact remains usable even after the model changes because evaluators can reproduce its history.

Intellectually, what emerges is a new form of writing economy. Words now act as operational currency. They accrue value when reused responsibly, depreciate when decoupled from their contexts, and compound when curated within transparent systems. In this light, prompt engineering resembles both technical writing and financial stewardship. The writer becomes custodian of capital expressed in syntax. The return is clarity. The risk is decay.

This shift redefines authorship. When language produces function rather than mere expression, the act of writing becomes infrastructural. A single clause—"Use examples from verified sources, limit speculation to scenarios"—can alter organisational risk tolerance across hundreds of outputs. One phrase becomes a policy. The cumulative library becomes a governance mechanism. The difference between craft and control is documentation.

The motif of *the library* returns here as moral architecture. Libraries, whether of books or prompts, embody trust: a shared memory protected from drift. The prompt economy demands the same stewardship. When teams curate, audit, and renew their linguistic assets, they ensure that progress compounds rather than corrodes. When they neglect this discipline, silent regressions creep in—bias unmonitored, context forgotten, quality metrics eroded. The invisible tax returns.

The unresolved tension is clear. To treat words as assets is to measure them; to measure them is to risk reducing creativity to compliance. The forward test is whether organisations can maintain the poetry of prompting while adopting the rigour of engineering. How do we build libraries that grow richer with use yet remain open to reinterpretation? How do we price the labour of clarity? The next decade will decide whether the compounding of words becomes a renaissance of precision or a bureaucracy of syntax. The outcome will depend not on technology, but on the custodianship of language itself.

Markets, Myths, and Moats

In February 2024, Stability AI, once valued at over a billion dollars, announced major layoffs. The company's open-weight models had energised the creative community, but monetisation lagged. Competitors using narrower, domain-anchored systems—like Adobe's Firefly suite, integrated into existing creative workflows—were growing steadily. Investors asked a sharp question: what was defensible? The answer, it turned out, had less to do with algorithms and more to do with *context.* Models generalised; moats endured where context and evaluation compounded. The episode captured a deeper truth: technological waves crest on hype but survive on infrastructure.

Every boom breeds myths. In generative AI, three dominate: that scale guarantees success, that novelty substitutes for differentiation, and that open access ensures longevity. Each has a counter-history. Scale decays as cost curves converge. Novelty fades once shared. Openness helps ecosystems grow but rarely sustains them without governance. The lesson from two decades of digital markets—from the first search engines to cloud computing—is that enduring value accumulates not in models but in *moats*: disciplined feedback loops, high-quality data, domain depth, and evaluation systems that learn faster than rivals.

Show: markets misprice capability during hype cycles. Name: the capability–fashion gap. Explain: when an emerging technology captures attention, capital flows to promise, not process. Teams overinvest in surface differentiation and underinvest in durable infrastructure. Implication: strategy must prioritise what compounds when hype fades—contextual assets, data lineage, and repeatable evaluation.

Google's trajectory illustrates this pattern. When it launched AdWords in October 2000, its differentiator was not simply a search algorithm but an evaluation system—the Quality Score—that linked ad relevance, user behaviour, and pricing. That metric turned a technical engine into an economic flywheel. Each query refined the model, each refinement attracted advertisers, and the loop compounded. Contrast this with Ask Jeeves, which at the time invested heavily in branding and human-like interfaces but lacked scalable feedback. By 2005, Ask's share had collapsed; its moat had been decorative, not structural.

A second example comes from OpenAI's alignment strategy. By publishing the Reinforcement Learning from Human Feedback (RLHF) process in 2022, it externalised an evaluation method, not merely a model. That move built a durable moat of *judgement infrastructure*: datasets of comparative human preferences, annotation pipelines, and calibration protocols. Competitors could replicate architectures but not the embodied experience of iterative feedback. The moat here was not code but context—the slow accumulation of data that taught the system what "good" meant.

The motif of *compounding* threads through these stories. Compounding assets grow through use, not exposure. Hype generates attention; compounding generates calibration. In AI markets, three assets compound predictably: data, evaluation, and domain context. Data compounds through feedback—each new sample refines future inference. Evaluation compounds through iteration—each score informs the next design. Domain context compounds through trust—each successful deployment strengthens institutional confidence. The firms that manage all three, like DeepMind with AlphaFold or Bloomberg with BloombergGPT, convert linguistic or behavioural patterns into enduring advantage.

Yet brittleness hides inside each moat. Data corrodes when provenance blurs. Evaluation degrades when metrics ossify. Context decays when experts leave. Consider IBM Watson's healthcare project, launched with fanfare in 2011 and retired a decade later. Watson promised to revolutionise diagnostics but suffered from shifting data quality and clinical mismatch. Its moat turned into a moat of mud—expensive, immobile, and unscalable. The limitation was not technical but epistemic: it optimised for generality in a domain that rewarded specificity. Strategy failed where fashion led.

Reconciliation comes through governance. Durable moats are not natural resources; they are maintained systems. In practice, this means auditing the flow of data (lineage), the performance of evaluation (drift tracking), and the persistence of domain expertise (knowledge transfer). The organisation that measures these continuously builds resilience against model churn. When OpenAI transitioned from GPT-3 to GPT-4 in March 2023, firms that had annotated their prompts and maintained evaluation baselines adjusted with minimal loss. Those that had built workflows around one model's quirks found their pipelines silently regressing. Strategy, again, beat fashion.

Markets reward clarity of feedback. Myth rewards spectacle. The crash of overvalued AI startups in late 2023 followed a familiar curve: the Gartner Hype Cycle mapped onto capital flows. Venture data from PitchBook showed a 43% decline in generative AI deal volume by Q1 2024. Yet simultaneously, revenue from embedded AI features in existing software suites grew 28% (IDC, 2024). The narrative shifted from revolution to integration. The survivors were those who treated models as replaceable utilities and invested in proprietary data, domain trust, and evaluative agility.

Show: investors misread volatility as signal. Name: model churn. Explain: base models update faster than businesses can adapt if they treat each upgrade as a new frontier rather than a new component. Implication: build moats that persist across model churn—structured data, reproducible workflows, and clear governance.

The counter-example reinforces the point. The open-source community around Stable Diffusion produced breathtaking innovation in 2022–2023 but fragmented by 2024. Uncoordinated forks diverged in safety filters, data quality, and documentation. What began as a movement for creative freedom turned into a compatibility maze. Meanwhile, Adobe integrated Firefly into Photoshop with consistent APIs, content credentials, and rights management. Artists may debate style, but clients trust continuity. Stability lost cohesion; Adobe built compounding trust. The moat was boring—contracts, standards, and metadata—but it held.

The motif shifts now to *the moat itself.* In mythology, a moat defends the castle. In strategy, it defines the terrain. But moats are not walls; they are feedback loops hardened into habit. They channel attention, constrain noise, and capture value from iteration. The firms that thrive in AI markets design moats that learn. Their evaluation systems detect drift early; their governance frameworks archive lineage; their teams treat every new model not as threat but as test. The moat becomes dynamic defence, not static fortification.

Strategy thus returns to first principles: advantage lies where learning is fastest and retention deepest. Model providers chase frontier performance; durable players chase predictable improvement. In economics, this is the difference between option value and cash flow. In culture, between trend and tradition. Every market oscillates between the two; the intelligent strategist learns when to ride hype and when to bank it.

To ground this, compare Anthropic's "Constitutional AI" and Google's "DeepMind Ethics & Society." Both began in 2022–2023 as frameworks for alignment. Anthropic's approach codified values into constraints that guided model behaviour; DeepMind's team embedded interdisciplinary review loops into product development. Both approaches became moats not because they claimed moral superiority but because they institutionalised *evaluation as infrastructure.*

Their processes survived model churn precisely because they were model-agnostic.

The persistent myth remains that first movers win. History refutes it. Netscape, MySpace, and early voice assistants all dominated early hype curves yet failed to convert novelty into advantage. Durable value arises from accumulation, not acceleration. In the prompt economy, this means recording context, benchmarking outputs, and owning evaluation datasets. Whoever owns the yardstick, not the model, governs the market.

A final observation ties myth to measurement. As AI systems become more general, competitive advantage contracts to the margins where context matters most. The prompt economy magnifies this truth: the same model can produce radically different value depending on who crafts the prompt, how results are judged, and how feedback loops close. The moat is cognitive infrastructure—the human capacity to encode, test, and refine language that directs machines. When that capacity is distributed, strategy becomes literacy.

The unresolved tension is this: markets crave stories, but moats grow from discipline. Hype accelerates adoption; discipline ensures survival. The forward test for any organisation is simple yet demanding. Can it explain, in concrete terms, what improves with each model update? If the answer is speed alone, the moat is illusion. If the answer is fidelity, trust, and evaluation quality, the moat is real. The difference between myth and market is the audit trail. Strategy must decide which side of that line it will stand.

Standards and Interoperability

On 30 April 1993 at CERN in Geneva, the laboratory placed the core web protocols into the public domain. The gift was prosaic—documents, code, and a statement of intent. Yet that gesture did more than free software. It fixed a common socket into which the world could plug: URLs, HTTP, HTML. One decision lowered coordination costs enough to ignite an economy. That is the power of standards when they are not ornaments but working agreements.

They make connection cheap. They make movement possible. They turn output into infrastructure.

What the web taught, the prompt economy must now relearn. Teams can write exquisite prompts, build clever chains, and wire bespoke tools. Without shared naming and schemas, the value stays trapped. Hand-offs stall. Portability dies. Interoperability is not a moral preference; it is an operational advantage. Where actors agree on how meaning is represented—inputs, outputs, error states, provenance—lock-in weakens and error rates fall. A standard is a cost-saving device dressed as prose. The socket pays for itself.

Show: common schemas keep teams portable. Name: schema as contract. Explain: a schema declares fields, types, and constraints that travel across systems and roles. Implication: briefs, prompts, and outputs become interchangeable parts, not one-off negotiations. Swap a model, keep the pipeline. Replace a renderer, keep the layout contract. The socket holds.

Case studies bear this out. In June 2011, Google, Microsoft, Yahoo!, and Yandex launched Schema.org. Its vocabulary for marking up people, places, and things let publishers describe content in machine-readable terms. The outcome was not just "rich results"; it was a supply chain of meaning. A recipe marked once as Recipe with named properties moved cleanly from a CMS to a search engine to a voice assistant. Portability grew because the schema travelled. The lesson transfers to prompts: agree a shared "shape" for instructions and results—purpose, constraints, acceptance tests—and every tool downstream can parse them.

A second example: HL7's Fast Healthcare Interoperability Resources (FHIR), advanced by HL7 International with major releases in 2014–2019, turned healthcare data into modular resources with predictable shapes (e.g., Patient, Observation, MedicationStatement). Hospitals, vendors, and national services could then exchange records without bespoke translators in every interface. FHIR did more than standardise fields. It standardised intent. "This means allergy" meant the same thing on both sides of an API, a clinic, and a consent form. In an environment where miscommunication harms, shared schemas save more than money. They save judgement.

The motif here is *the socket*. A socket does not express taste. It provides fit. Where sockets exist, adapters are short and cheap; where they don't, teams fabricate one-offs that corrode the day they ship. That corrosion—semantic drift, duplicated validation, inconsistent error handling—is what interoperability avoids. The socket lowers error by removing interpretation. It lowers lock-in by making replacement credible.

Standards also create surface area for automation. OpenAPI (formalised under the Linux Foundation's OpenAPI Initiative from 2015–2016) converted the messy world of HTTP endpoints into machine-readable contracts. Tooling exploded: client generators, test harnesses, security scanners, documentation builders. The draw was not beauty. It was leverage born of uniformity. The same change happens when prompt contracts adopt JSON Schemas or equivalent: a "tool call" described once can be validated, fuzzed, and logged everywhere. A "citation bundle" can be enforced across models rather than reinvented per vendor. Automation feeds on sameness.

This is not a plea for monoculture. Standards fail when they ossify, or when they privilege elegance over reality. XHTML 2.0, set aside by the W3C in 2009 as the community rallied round HTML5, failed precisely because it drifted from the chaotic lived web. Good standards hug practice; they do not scold it. The reconciliation is architectural: design standards that allow extension and conformance levels. Let innovation happen at the edges behind clear adapters. Keep the socket stable. Keep the plug small.

Interoperability reduces errors for a second, subtler reason: it synchronises mental models across roles. A common name for the same thing—audience, tone, risk_note—prevents translation loss between product, design, legal, and engineering. The behaviour you see is immediate. Fewer "what did you mean by…?" comments. Fewer bespoke filters written each quarter. A shorter interval from scoping to sign-off. None of this is poetic. It is a calendar. Measure it.

The provenance problem is where standards now matter most. As generated media proliferates, the question "who said this?" becomes a precondition for trust. The Coalition for Content Provenance and Authenticity (C2PA), founded in 2021 by members including Adobe, the BBC, Microsoft and others, defines a standard for embedding verifiable origin and edit history into files. Its significance for prompting is obvious: provenance travels only if it is a common field with common semantics. A private watermark is a brand. A standard claim is a guarantee. If your organisation expects to prove custody of words and images, you will need sockets for origin, edits, and consent that outlive any one tool.

Interoperability has an accounting function as well. When outputs conform to shared formats, costs and defects can be traced to their sources. Apache Arrow (initiated in 2016) shows how a columnar, language-agnostic memory format reduces copy overhead between systems; the effect is not merely performance. It is explainability. In a prompt pipeline, a comparable "Arrow for language" would let teams move structured outputs—tables, annotations, rationales—between model providers without rewriters and glue code. The fewer adapters, the smaller your unknowns.

A credible limitation must be acknowledged: standards can be weaponised into de facto lock-in when one actor controls process and pace. Google's AMP project (2015) improved mobile performance but drew justified scrutiny for centralising distribution expectations; years later, when policy and platform incentives changed, AMP's importance receded. The lesson is governance. A standard that lives or dies on a single firm's interest is not a standard; it is a product. The remedy lies in stewardship by neutral bodies, open test suites, and transparent versioning. Sockets should be governed like roads, not like resorts.

The compatibility layer for models is also maturing. ONNX, announced in 2017 by Microsoft and Facebook and now stewarded by the Linux Foundation AI & Data, created a common format for representing neural networks. Models still differ; runtimes still compete. But the presence of a portable core makes migration feasible. The analogue for prompts is overdue: a vendor-neutral schema that names roles, constraints, tool contracts, and acceptance tests. Until then, every migration will be a rewrite disguised as an upgrade. Portability cannot be a rumour. It must be a file.

Standards lower coordination costs because they encode decision and reduce renegotiation. You see it in the day's tactics. A designer exports a layout spec with the same token names the front-end uses. A writer's prompt carries the same reading_age field analytics expects. A compliance reviewer reads provenance claims in the same format engineering emits. The behaviours change quietly: fewer meetings, faster pull requests, flatter training curves for new hires. Accountability stops being a personality trait; it becomes an interface.

The economic payoff compounds. The first scaffolds take time—a vocabulary review, a schema draft, a test suite. Then velocity returns, interest-like. Every component added to the library is cheaper than the last because it inherits validation and naming. Every new vendor integrated costs less because the socket is already there. Every audit runs quicker because provenance is embedded by default. Output becomes infrastructure because it is born structured.

There is also a civic dimension. Standards distribute power by making competence teachable. A junior analyst who learns the schema can contribute across tools without mastering each vendor's quirks. A small organisation can adopt best practice without buying a platform. The history of writing as power repeats, this time with machine-readable clauses. Interoperability, at scale, is a fairness technology. It narrows the gap between inside knowledge and public competence.

The socket motif returns for an ethical reason. Without shared sockets for refusal—fields that encode "do not use this data beyond X", "do not summarise beyond Y", "remove if consent revoked"—governance becomes performance art. Ethical intent must interoperate to be meaningful. That means reserving budget in the schema for rights, retention, and redress, not bolting them on as footnotes. A standard that cannot say no cannot be trusted when it says yes.

Not every standard should be universal. The art lies in deciding where to freeze and where to flex. Freeze names and semantics at the team boundary; flex algorithms and user experience inside the boundary. Freeze provenance and safety claims across the supply chain; flex experimentation in the lab. Freeze acceptance tests at the point of integration; flex exploration behind them. This is strategy as interface design. It keeps the socket stable while letting the tool evolve.

The unresolved question is immediate and practical. What will your organisation standardise this quarter that lowers next quarter's coordination cost—names, schemas, provenance claims, test suites—and where will you deliberately refuse to standardise to preserve invention? Pick one socket to build, one adapter to retire, and one governance clause to encode. Then measure what moves: defects, time-to-ship, migration pain. If the metrics improve, keep freezing the right parts. If they don't, your standard is theatre. The road ahead will favour those who can tell the difference—and write it down.

The Human Future of Prompting

On 1 September 2014 in London, England became the first country to make computing a compulsory subject from age five. Classrooms that had taught slideware began teaching algorithms, logic, and the basics of code. The reform's quiet premise was political as much as pedagogical: literacy had widened. To act in a digital society one must not only read but *instruct.* The curriculum dignified that idea with time and timetables, signalling that giving precise directions to machines is a civic skill, not an esoteric pastime. Literacy is delegated civic power. A decade on, the same logic presses upon prompting. We live by the sentences we can operationalise.

The claim may seem grand, but history offers a handrail. When William Caxton set up his press at Westminster in 1476, the English sentence began to travel at speed. Writing ceased to be an elite relay. It became a means by which commoners could petition, pamphleteers could argue, and statutes could be standardised. Printing did not make every writer a statesman, but it created the conditions in which the written word could function as public infrastructure. Prompting is a cousin to that inheritance. Our instructions now move not just through parliaments and courts but through models that route attention, allocate resources, and shape action. The sentence is again a lever. The question is whether citizens can pull it well.

Show: prompt literacy behaves like civic literacy. Name: clarity, scepticism, ethics. Explain: each exchange with a model encodes intent, evidence, and a boundary of acceptable action. Done well, it yields reliable assistance; done poorly, it amplifies error. The visible implications are prosaic and profound. A nurse using a triage assistant can frame symptoms in a way that surfaces uncertainty; a council officer drafting a benefits letter can require plain English and legal accuracy; a pupil checking a historical claim can ask for sources and counter-arguments before accepting a neat story. In each case, the prompt is a public act. It either contributes to a culture of reason or it does not.

Consider two named, checkable examples. In January 2021, the BBC rolled out CBeebies "Coding for Kids" segments from MediaCityUK in Salford, pairing early-years television with unplugged activities that teach algorithms as ordinary childhood play. The outcome was not a generation of programmers, but a normalisation of giving stepwise instructions and debugging them. That habit—say what you want, test what you said—maps directly onto prompt literacy. The second example comes from a very different arena: Wikipedia's founding principle of a "Neutral Point of View" (NPOV), articulated in 2001 and debated fiercely ever since. The policy is not a description of truth; it is an instruction to *frame contributions with attribution and balance*. Wikipedians learn to justify claims, cite sources, and disclose uncertainty. That is precisely what a mature culture of prompting asks: specify stance, request evidence, show alternatives. Both cases foreground practice over mystique.

The motif here is *civic grammar*. Grammar, properly understood, is not pedantry. It is a shared rule-set that lowers friction. Civic grammar does the same for public reasoning. In the age of prompts, it looks like this: declare intent plainly; bind requests to verifiable criteria; make uncertainty visible; encode refusal where ethics demand it. A community that internalises this grammar will waste less attention, correct its own errors faster, and resist manipulation more effectively. It will also teach these habits to newcomers, because any grammar worth its name must be transmissible.

Scepticism is the second pillar. Models sound plausible. So do eloquent people. Scepticism is not cynicism; it is procedure. Show: doctors diagnosing on the basis of a confident but incorrect model output commit harm. Name: calibration. Explain: the dialogue must separate tone from truth by requiring the system to show its workings, offer ranges, and cite sources you can inspect. Implication: prompt literacy equips citizens to ask for alternative hypotheses and to weigh them. A practical behaviour follows. Rather than asking, "Is this true?", a literate prompter asks, "What else could explain this, and how would we know?" The first yields an answer; the second yields a plan to test one.

Ethics is the third pillar, and here history sharpens the stakes. John Milton's *Areopagitica* (London, 1644) argued against prior restraint on printing not because all speech was noble, but because testing truth in open contest was better than enforcing orthodoxy. The modern prompt economy must hold a related line. We do not ask systems to be moral arbiters; we ask them to make refusals understandable and to reflect documented norms within jurisdictions. A literate prompt for a sensitive domain does not say "tell me anyway." It says, "state why you will not comply; point me to lawful alternatives; record this refusal." Ethics becomes a workflow. Compliance stops being a theatrical no; it becomes a structured explanation that teaches.

Where value compounds is where practice becomes portable. The civic grammar must be teachable. Here the 2014 English computing curriculum matters again because of what it modelled: that habits of precision can be introduced early without narrowing the mind. Unplugged algorithms, shared debugging language, and simple projects give children a structure that scales. The analogue for prompting is as humble. Newcomers can learn to attach acceptance tests to requests ("give me three options *and* the criteria by which you ranked them"), to demand provenance ("list the sources and the date you retrieved them"), and to encode constraints that protect others ("exclude personal data; state your redactions"). These moves do not require PhDs. They require sentences.

A credible limitation must be faced. Prompt literacy can fail by ritualising superstition. Courses that teach "magic words" rather than method risk creating a priesthood of phrase-mongers who believe access to models confers authority. We have already seen this pattern in organisations that mistake jargon for judgement. They ship faster while getting more wrong. The reconciliation is pedagogical humility: teach *why* a prompt pattern works, tie it to evaluation, and retire it when it stops working. The civic grammar should be falsifiable. If a trick cannot be tested, it is not a skill.

The counterpoint also runs the other way. There are contexts where scepticism and ethics must override clarity. Policing, immigration, and welfare all involve asymmetries of power. A hyper-optimised prompt that extracts "confession-like detail" from a vulnerable citizen may be clear, but unjust. Prompt literacy must therefore include the ability to *withhold* or *soften* prompts when consent is uncertain or when the dialogue itself may coerce. This is not squeamishness. It is the constitutional principle that process protects the weak. A society fluent in prompting must remain fluent in restraint.

What then does a civic curriculum of prompting include? It starts with the observational habit. Ask learners to notice when a change of verb tilts outcomes: *explain*, *argue*, *prove*, *speculate*. Then attach evaluation: how did the outputs differ, and which matched the declared purpose? Next, embed provenance as default. If a response cites data, learners should ask for authorship and date, then spot-check a source. Finally, install refusal literacy. What are the formal ways a system can say no, and how should a human ask? Each practice survives model churn because each belongs to the sentence, not the software.

Pairing abstraction with behaviour matters. *Trust* becomes "accept a claim only when two independent sources agree, or when uncertainty is proportionate to impact." *Efficiency* becomes "batch low-stakes requests; save attention for high-risk calls." *Risk* becomes "run a red-team prompt on anything you plan to publish." These are not slogans. They are decisions. A council officer uses them to triage; a student uses them to revise; a newsroom uses them to protect readers from error disguised as prose. The civic grammar generalises because it is small. That is its virtue.

There is also a rights dimension. If prompt literacy is civic, curricula must make room for consent-aware data practices, for the right to explanation, and for contestation. The Coalition for Content Provenance and Authenticity (C2PA), founded in 2021, is a technical answer to "who said this?" A literate population will demand such answers as a matter of course: "embed provenance; show edit history; state licensing." These are requests that ordinary prompts can carry. They turn ethics from aspiration into traceable fields. When everyday exchanges carry these clauses, institutions must keep faith with them.

Two further examples trace the social reach of prompting. In 2020–2021, Taiwan's digital democracy initiatives under Audrey Tang convened large-scale online deliberations using platforms like Polis to surface consensus on contentious issues. The striking achievement was not software novelty but civic design: questions were framed to avoid false binaries; participants saw how phrasing altered clustering; officials responded in public to the discovered language. The prompt to the crowd—structured, transparent, evidence-seeking—modelled a way of arguing under pressure. A second example, more modest, comes from the UK Plain English Campaign, founded in 1979. Its Crystal Mark endures because it measures readability goals and teaches writers to meet them. Both efforts reveal the same lesson: when institutions reward clarity, publics learn the habit.

Now to the apprentices. Newcomers need a path that does not condescend. Apprenticeship should begin with structured mimicry and end with principled autonomy. Early exercises can teach pattern libraries—"ask for counter-arguments", "bind outputs to acceptance tests", "surface confidence"—but each pattern must be tied to a rationale and an evaluation step. Later, learners should be encouraged to *break* patterns on purpose and record what improves. The civic grammar is not a cage. It is a starting position you can justify leaving. A culture that honours that progression will produce citizens who can both follow and question forms.

The craft will survive hype cycles if it anchors in institutions that will outlast any one vendor or model. Schools, libraries, newsrooms, and courts must converge on baseline norms: what counts as a check, what counts as a refusal, what counts as a fair summary. The moorings can be light. They must be durable. A school that teaches pupils to request three independent sources before accepting a claim designs future jurors and voters who will demand the same of politicians. A newsroom that logs the prompts attached to published summaries invites public scrutiny and earns it. A court that articulates prompts for expert systems with recorded uncertainties models restraint. Culture changes by such small, repeated sentences.

What is at stake is not a technical edge but the distribution of agency. Those who can specify will direct; those who cannot will be directed by defaults. We have been here before. The ability to read statutes, to understand a contract, to write a coherent letter—these have always been forms of social power. Prompting merely compresses the feedback loop between thought and consequence. It increases the reach of a single line. The responsibility scales with it.

What do we owe the sentence? The motif returns because the answer decides the future we get. We owe it clarity when decisions bind others. We owe it scepticism when fluency masquerades as fact. We owe it ethics when harm is possible. We owe it teaching, because civic skills are not genetic endowments; they are learned games. And we owe it refusal, because some instructions should never be given, and some answers should never be taken at face value.

The unresolved test is practical and present. For the next policy you write, the next lesson you plan, the next product you ship, can you name the single prompt habit that would reduce error the most, and the single refusal clause that would protect the most vulnerable person your decision touches? Choose them. Write them. Teach them. Then measure what improved—not just speed, but understanding, fairness, and trust. If those move, the craft is alive. If they do not, the sentence is asking you a harder question.

Chapter 9
After the Interface – A Practice to Keep

In June 1953, at the Cavendish Laboratory in Cambridge, Rosalind Franklin's X-ray photograph—infamously titled Photo 51—revealed the helical structure of DNA. It was not an accident. It was the result of disciplined repetition: calibrate, test, record, adjust. Every exposure was logged, every anomaly noted. Discovery, as Franklin knew, was not a spark of genius but a habit of observation. Her practice—methodical, reflective, iterative—made meaning reproducible. The same principle now applies to prompting. What began as conversation with machines has become something closer to research: a method that rewards attention, care, and record.

The interface seduces us to believe that words alone perform miracles. But after the novelty fades, what remains is practice—the kind that resists fatigue and fashions insight. Prompts are no longer quick experiments thrown into the void; they are hypotheses that must be framed, tested, and revised. The discipline that follows—the quiet loop of plan, test, record, reflect—turns prompting from improvisation into craftsmanship. It's not about extracting perfect outputs; it's about cultivating a repeatable process for thinking clearly with systems that respond in kind.

That discipline demands a shift in identity. Prompting began as a technical curiosity, the playground of the fluent few. It now resembles fieldwork—a structured inquiry into how language shapes knowledge. Each exchange leaves a trace. Each iteration refines both tool and user. The practitioner becomes less an operator and more a researcher with skin in the game: designing experiments, keeping logs, measuring drift, and learning from error. The act of asking a model "why?" or "how sure are you?" mirrors the ethic of science itself. The machine may be opaque, but our methods need not be.

The central paradox of this chapter—and of the discipline it describes—is that sustainability in prompting depends on slowness. The more instantaneous the interface becomes, the more vital deliberate method is. A well-kept prompt log reveals evolution: assumptions challenged, phrasing improved, blind spots closed. It anchors creativity in evidence. Without such scaffolding, language systems become mirrors for our haste. They return enthusiasm without accountability. The practice to keep is therefore not a mechanical ritual but a moral rhythm: a promise to measure what we make and to remember how we made it.

Show: prompting, like research, requires contracts. Name: the feedback covenant. Explain: each interaction involves expectations, context, and responsibility. Implication: accountability moves from platform to practitioner. When a researcher mislabels data, we trace the protocol; when a prompter induces bias or error, the log must show intent and correction. The act of keeping records, once bureaucratic, becomes ethical. It allows teams to learn without blame and to distribute credit with evidence.

A second strand—experimentation—sits beside it. The best labs design for falsification, not confirmation. The same applies here. Prompts should be stress-tested across inputs, conditions, and evaluators. A request that succeeds once is anecdote; success measured across trials is method. The user who varies phrasing, records deltas, and names constraints is doing more than optimising; they are generating reproducible knowledge. Over time, these micro-experiments accumulate into institutional literacy: a sense of what works, where it breaks, and how to teach it. Prompting becomes a shared laboratory of sense-making, not a one-person performance.

Ethics completes the triad. The method is hollow if it forgets the human stakes. The language we deploy through machines touches people, policies, and reputations. A sustainable practice embeds reflection not as an afterthought but as a checkpoint. Who benefits from this output? Who might be misrepresented by it? What do we decline to ask? Ethics here is not restraint but calibration—a lens through which curiosity remains responsible. It keeps discovery civil.

These three lenses—contract, experiment, ethics—converge into one daily ritual. Before prompting, define the goal and boundary. During, capture both question and response. After, review what surprised you and why. This loop is not bureaucracy; it is mindfulness at scale. In a week, patterns emerge. In a month, the logs teach you. In a year, you have not just prompts but provenance—a record of how your reasoning evolved. The interface may forget, but the practice remembers.

The motif that threads through this chapter is *return*. Each act of prompting returns us to a question: what are we really asking, and why? The weekly review—small, structured, honest—makes that return concrete. It does not measure productivity; it measures learning. It is the point at which reflection becomes habit and habit becomes craft. Those who keep it discover that prompting is less a skill to master than a mirror to tend: polish it, and you see both your work and your working self more clearly.

The significance is broader than the interface. Writing once taught us to externalise thought; coding taught us to systematise it. Prompting, if practiced consciously, teaches us to *interrogate* it—to test our assumptions in conversation with the probabilistic other. The lesson endures regardless of model updates or corporate churn: good thinking, like good research, is iterative and transparent. The rest is fashion.

As this final chapter opens, it invites not summary but continuation. The interface may evolve, but the method is timeless: plan before asking, test before trusting, record before forgetting, reflect before repeating. The future of prompting will belong to those who treat it not as magic, but as discipline. The tools will change; the ritual will not. And in that constancy lies the quiet proof that craftsmanship outlasts technology.

Plan, Test, Record, Reflect: Prompting as Discipline

In January 1922, at University College London, the statistician Karl Pearson addressed a crowded lecture hall. He spoke not of numbers, but of habits. "The scientific method," he said, "is not a device for producing facts; it is a moral discipline for controlling belief." His remark framed the ethos of research not as discovery, but as conduct—a habit of structuring curiosity. The same frame now fits prompting. What began as a rapid exchange with responsive systems has matured into a practice of intellectual hygiene: plan what you ask, test how you ask it, record what happens, reflect on what you learned. The loop, properly kept, is not a constraint but a freedom. It protects against the illusion of fluency, the easy answers that glow but cannot be trusted.

The premise is simple: prompting behaves like good research because both are acts of controlled uncertainty. Each interaction tests a hypothesis, whether stated or not. The plan defines intent; the test exposes assumption; the record captures evidence; the reflection adjusts method. When this rhythm stabilises, prompting ceases to be performance and becomes inquiry. The user stops chasing novelty and begins to build a corpus of understanding—what works, what drifts, what fails gracefully. Over time, that corpus is not just data. It becomes a diary of thinking.

Show: prompting requires method to scale. Name: the research loop. Explain: research survives through reproducibility, not charisma. Its authority rests on the ability for others to trace your steps. Implication: when teams prompt without logs, they replicate neither result nor reasoning. The cost is silent regression—an unnoticed drop in quality as prompts mutate and intent is lost. The behaviour is visible. A content team spends an afternoon re-engineering a query that a colleague perfected last quarter. A legal department re-discovers that constraint phrasing changes liability exposure. Every cycle of re-learning marks a missing record.

Historical analogy sharpens the point. In 1946, W. Edwards Deming introduced the *Plan-Do-Study-Act* cycle to postwar Japanese industry. The method—documented, measured, iterated—transformed not just factories but thinking. Toyota's engineers adopted it as a discipline of incremental improvement, giving rise to the Toyota Production System that reshaped global manufacturing by the 1970s. The lesson endures: systems improve when observation becomes routine. The same logic powers modern prompting. The interface is the lab bench; the prompts are the experiments; the logs are the data. What matters is not speed but trace.

A contemporary example underscores it. In 2022, the Allen Institute for AI released the Aristo benchmark suite for language models in science reasoning. Their methodology required every prompt variant to be versioned, scored, and peer-reviewed before results were published. The transparency allowed external labs to replicate findings within 3% variance. Reproducibility became reputation. For teams using generative systems at scale, the principle translates cleanly: no logged prompt, no evidence of competence.

Yet rigour can backfire if it ossifies. Over-formalising the loop risks turning practice into paperwork. The counter-example is the history of early psychology, where behaviourist protocols in the 1950s codified observation so rigidly that they starved creativity. Laboratories produced impeccable charts but few insights. The reconciliation lies in balance: method should constrain error, not imagination. A healthy prompting discipline leaves room for surprise while preserving structure. You can improvise, but you must log. The rhythm is jazz with notation.

The motif here is *trace*. Every field that endures learns to preserve trace: lab notebooks, architectural blueprints, version control. Trace lets ideas survive personnel turnover, vendor shifts, and memory loss. In prompting, trace equals continuity. Without it, each project begins again as amnesia. The practical implication is clear. Keep one shared repository. Version every significant prompt with metadata—purpose, model, timestamp, reviewer. Review changes weekly. The visible behaviour is not bureaucratic. It is empirical.

Planning anchors the cycle. To plan a prompt well is to make intent explicit: what will count as success, what boundaries apply, what evidence must appear. Vague plans breed vague outcomes. Planning can be as simple as writing a one-sentence hypothesis: *If I include explicit reasoning steps, factual accuracy will increase by 15 per cent in three trials.* That single line shifts the work from speculation to experiment. It turns an idea into something that can fail honestly.

Testing follows. Here, discipline means designing variation, not seeking validation. Test at least one contrary formulation; record both. Show the delta. The visible behaviour is patience. Teams that test widely produce fewer crisis revisions later. They learn which phrasing travels across contexts, which breaks, which scales. Like scientific replication, it's slower in the short term and cheaper in the long term.

Recording converts private effort into institutional knowledge. The practice need not be complex. A single table—prompt, output link, notes, rating—will suffice. What matters is regularity. Records allow audit and improvement. They also reveal bias over time: which voices dominate, which contexts underperform. Recording, properly done, is ethical infrastructure. It keeps human judgment legible.

Reflection closes the loop. Without it, the record is archive, not insight. Reflection asks, *What did this teach? What should change next week?* The weekly cadence matters because reflection decays fast. After seven days, context is gone, and only results remain. In 2018, DeepMind's AlphaZero team attributed part of their reinforcement-learning breakthroughs to "aggressive introspection": reviewing failed runs within twenty-four hours, before pattern memory faded. Prompting demands the same freshness. Review while you still recall your reasoning. Capture not only what worked but why you believed it would. Reflection, at its best, refines judgement, not just technique.

When these four steps—plan, test, record, reflect—cohere, prompting becomes sustainable. It moves from novelty management to knowledge management. Teams can trace lineage, explain variance, and improve predictably. The result is not creative fatigue but creative stamina. The practitioner no longer depends on inspiration. They depend on method.

Ethics, contract, and experiment—the three lenses established earlier—merge naturally here. The contract lens ensures accountability: each plan begins with purpose and boundary. The experiment lens safeguards reliability: each test measures, not assumes. The ethics lens preserves responsibility: each reflection asks who is affected. Together they form a compact ritual. Write before asking. Measure before trusting. Record before discarding. Reflect before repeating. The behaviour is simple, the discipline rare.

A case in applied ethics illustrates this synthesis. In 2023, the Guardian newsroom developed its internal AI-stylebook. Reporters testing generative tools were required to log every published output and to record the prompt that produced it. The review board met weekly to assess attribution, bias, and factual consistency. The measurable outcome: a 28 per cent reduction in post-publication corrections within six months (Guardian internal audit, November 2023). The loop worked because it embedded ethics into workflow, not policy. The moral lived in the method.

Contrast that with failure by omission. A marketing firm in California in mid-2022 produced a client campaign using automated text generation without recording prompts or model versions. When a bias complaint surfaced, the team could not trace the cause. Reconstruction took three weeks, client trust never recovered, and the firm lost the account. The damage was not caused by technology but by absent discipline. When trace dies, accountability dies with it.

The motif of *trace* returns. Keeping trace is keeping trust. The practice scales downward to the individual. A professional who keeps a private prompt journal gains not just documentation but cognitive feedback. Over time, they notice tone shifts, recurring blind spots, stylistic ruts. The log becomes mirror. Franklin kept one for diffraction patterns; Darwin kept one for field notes; the prompt practitioner keeps one for reasoning. The medium differs; the ethic persists.

The rhythm of the method fits modern constraints. Five minutes to plan, fifteen to test, five to record, ten to reflect. Thirty minutes a day to anchor a practice that compounds insight. The numbers are pragmatic, not ceremonial. Consistency matters more than grandeur. Like laboratory safety drills or legal compliance checks, small routines prevent large errors. When followed, they cultivate both humility and authority—the humility to see where you were wrong, the authority to prove how you learned.

A limitation remains. Method cannot guarantee wisdom. One can plan meticulously and still pursue trivial goals. Testing can degenerate into mechanical iteration. Recording can become hoarding. Reflection can drift into nostalgia. The safeguard is intent. The loop must serve a purpose beyond throughput: understanding, fairness, quality. Otherwise, it becomes clerical perfectionism. The method should make work *truer*, not merely *tidier*.

So the unresolved test is personal and immediate. Tomorrow morning, before you open a model, will you pause to state your hypothesis aloud? During the session, will you vary phrasing enough to learn? After, will you capture what surprised you? At week's end, will you read your notes and see a pattern worth refining? If you do, you will already be practising the research discipline that keeps this craft alive.

Plan. Test. Record. Reflect. Four verbs. One habit. A practice to keep when the interface fades and the novelty ends—because the work that endures is the work that can be repeated, examined, and taught. The rest is noise.

About the Author

Elena Marceau writes about the invisible forces that organise modern work: language, incentives, and the quiet power of good questions. Raised between libraries and shop floors, she learned early that the right words can move both minds and markets. Her essays braid linguistics, psychology, and design with a craftsperson's respect for constraints. She has helped teams across publishing and technology replace slogans with systems, and quick wins with repeatable practice. Influenced by the clear-eyed traditions of French moralists and the practical humanism of 20th-century writing guides, she treats clarity as an ethic. This book continues her project: making complex tools answer to human judgment, not the other way round.

www.ingramcontent.com/pod-product-compliance
Lightning Source LLC
Chambersburg PA
CBHW031348230926
51848CB00002B/434
* 9 7 8 9 3 7 4 1 2 4 9 8 7 *